THE WEST HIGHLAND WAY

About the Author

Terry Marsh is a full-time writer and photographer specialising in the outdoors and travel in the UK, Ireland and France. He first visited Scotland in 1968, and has been returning ever since to write about and photograph its magnificent landscapes. His contributions to the literature of Scotland earned him a Fellowship of the Society of Antiquaries of Scotland. He is also a Fellow of the Royal Geographic Society, and holds a Master of Arts degree in Lake District Studies and a PhD in Historical Geography, both from the University of Lancaster.

Based in Lancashire, Terry continues his forays into Scotland on a regular basis, and has written guidebooks not only to the West Highland Way but to Southern Scotland, Edinburgh and the Lothians, Glasgow, the Isle of Skye, the Isle of Mull, and all the Scottish islands.

Terry is the author of a number of titles for Cicerone, in addition to the Skye and Mull books, covering the Isle of Man, the Coast-to-Coast Path, the Dales Way, Snowdonia, the Pennines and the modern leisure pursuit of geocaching.

Other Cicerone guides by the author

THE WEST HIGHLAND WAY

by Terry Marsh

JUNIPER HOUSE, MURLEY MOSS,
OXENHOLME ROAD, KENDAL, CUMBRIA LA9 7RL
www.cicerone.co.uk

Printed in China on behalf of Latitude Press Ltd
A catalogue record for this book is available from the British Library.
All photographs are by the author unless otherwise stated.

1:100K route mapping by Route mapping by Lovell Johns
www.lovelljohns.com. © Crown copyright 2016
OS PU100012932. NASA relief data courtesy of ESRI

The 1:25k map booklet contains Ordnance Survey data
© Crown copyright and database rights 2016
OS PU100012932.

Acknowledgments

The process of writing a book such as this is inordinately more complex (I hope) than the act of following the walk. But it is a task made considerably easier by an increasingly rare breed of individual who actually doesn't mind helping people along – in my case by the simple expedient of providing companionship along the way. I'd like to thank Ron and Tom for their company, always appreciated, between Crianlarich and Fort William during the first run; and my son Martin who accompanied me during the whole of the second visit. And when I came to revisit the Way twice in 2010, I was accompanied by my brother-in-law, Jon, who was excellent company and always ready to partake of whatever malt whiskies were on offer.

Front cover: Black Rock Cottage, Glencoe (Stage 5)

CONTENTS

Updates to this Guide

While every effort is made by our authors to ensure the accuracy of guidebooks as they go to print, changes can occur during the lifetime of an edition. Any updates that we know of for this guide will be on the Cicerone website (www.cicerone.co.uk/857/updates), so please check before planning your trip. We also advise that you check information about such things as transport, accommodation and shops locally. Even rights of way can be altered over time.

If you find accommodation listed here that is closed or unwelcoming to walkers, or know of suitable accommodation that we have left out, please let us know. Similarly, if you are an accommodation provider who would like adding to the list, or taking off the list, do get in touch. The most up-to-date version of Appendix B, based on reader feedback, can be downloaded from www.cicerone.co.uk/857/accommodation.

We are always grateful for information about any discrepancies between a guidebook and the facts on the ground, sent by email to updates@cicerone.co.uk or by post to Cicerone, Juniper House, Murley Moss, Oxenholme Road, Kendal LA9 7RL.

Register your book: To sign up to receive free updates, special offers and GPX files where available, register your book at www.cicerone.co.uk.

Symbols on the route maps

route

seasonal variant

alternative route

(S) start point

(F) finish point

Route map relief

400m
300m
200m
100m

0 kilometres 1 2

0 miles 1

SCALE: 1:100,000

Contour lines are drawn at
50m intervals and labelled
at 100m intervals.

Features on the overview map

———— County/Unitary boundary

———— National boundary

Urban area

National Park eg *Cairngorms*

Area of Outstanding Natural
Beauty eg *Ben Nevis & Glen Coe*

Overview map relief

>800m
600m
400m
200m
75m
0m

See 1:25,000 map booklet for the key to the 1:25,000 maps

The River Fillan in a gentle frame of mind

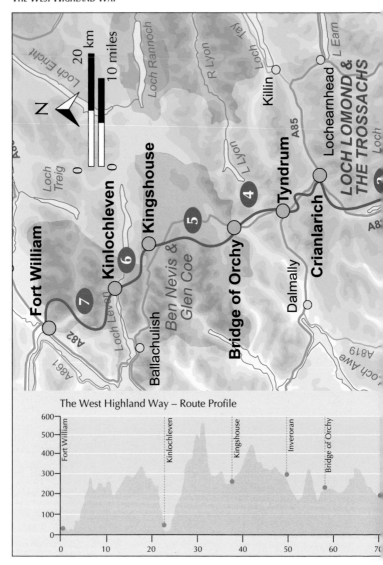

The West Highland Way – Route Profile

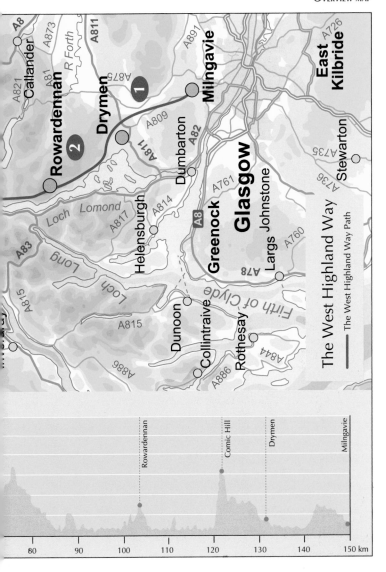

The West Highland Way

— The West Highland Way Path

The West Highland Way Trek Planner

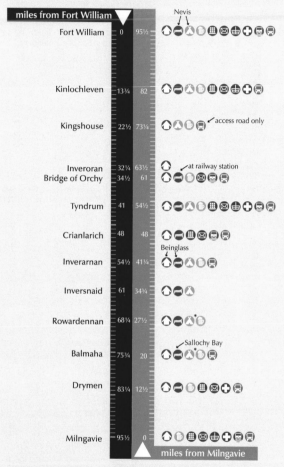

miles from Fort William		miles from Milngavie	
Fort William	0	95½	Nevis
Kinlochleven	13¾	82	
Kingshouse	22½	73¼	access road only
Inveroran	32¼	63½	
Bridge of Orchy	34½	61	at railway station
Tyndrum	41	54½	
Crianlarich	48	48	
Inverarnan	54½	41¼	Beinglass
Inversnaid	61	34¾	
Rowardennan	68¼	27½	
Balmaha	75¾	20	Sallochy Bay
Drymen	83¼	12½	
Milngavie	95½	0	

Hotel/B&B ⬠ Hostel/Bunkhouse ⬤ Camping* ⬠ Pub/Inn ⬤ Bank/ATM ⬛ Post Office ✉ Gear shop ⬤ Medical services ✚ Railway station ⬛ Public transport ⬛

⬠ * It is an offence to camp, sleep outdoors or in a vehicle in the East Loch Lomond Restricted Zone from 1 March to 31 October every year outside the designated sites located at Milarrochy, Cashel and Sallochy. View information and download a map at www.lochlomond-trossachs.org/visiting/east-loch-lomond-camping-byelaws/menu-id-611.html.

ROUTE SUMMARY TABLE: SOUTH TO NORTH

Stage	Start/Finish	Distance miles (km)	Ascent ft (m)	Descent ft (m)	Time hrs	Page
1	Milngavie/ Drymen	12½ (20)	835 (255)	845 (257)	5½–6	**42**
2	Drymen/ Rowardennan	15 (24)	2095 (638)	2215 (675)	6–7	**57**
3	Rowardennan/ Crianlarich	20 (32.5)	3330 (1015)	2790 (850)	10–12	**72**
4	Crianlarich/ Bridge of Orchy	13¼ (21.3)	1515 (462)	1590 (484)	7	**86**
5	Bridge of Orchy/ Kingshouse	12 (19.4)	1615 (493)	1335 (407)	5–6	**97**
6	Kingshouse/ Kinlochleven	8¾ (14)	1525 (465)	2290 (697)	4–5	**108**
7	Kinlochleven/ Fort William	14 (22)	2325 (710)	2325 (710)	7–8	**116**
Total		**95½ (153.2)**	**13,240 (4038)**	**13,390 (4080)**	**44½–51**	

ROUTE SUMMARY TABLE: NORTH TO SOUTH

Stage	Start/Finish	Distance miles (km)	Ascent ft (m)	Descent ft (m)	Time hrs	Page
1	Fort William/ Kinlochleven	14 (22)	2325 (725)	2325 (725)	7–8	**124**
2	Kinlochleven/ Kingshouse	8¾ (14)	2290 (697)	1525 (465)	4–5	**114**
3	Kingshouse/ Bridge of Orchy	12 (19.4)	1335 (407)	1615 (493)	5–6	**106**
4	Bridge of Orchy/ Crianlarich	13¼ (21.3)	1590 (484)	1515 (462)	7	**94**
5	Crianlarich/ Rowardennan	20 (32.5)	2790 (850)	3330 (850)	9–10	**84**
6	Rowardennan/ Drymen	15 (24)	2215 (675)	2095 (638)	6–7	**69**
7	Drymen/ Milngavie	12½ (20)	845 (257)	835 (255)	5½–6	**55**
Total		**95½ (153.2)**	**13,390 (4095)**	**13,240 (3888)**	**43½–49**	

PREFACE

Fine views over Loch Lomond (photo: Jonathan Williams)

When Walt Unsworth (the then owner of Cicerone Press) rang me to ask whether I could shelve the eternally ongoing encyclopaedia of the countryside I was working on for him and go off to do a guidebook to the West Highland Way, I confess I delayed my response by a good two nanoseconds, not wanting to appear too eager. But, I thought, if I don't do it, Walt will only get someone else to sort it out, so why not? It isn't every day you get a publisher throwing work your way – usually you have to grovel a bit first!

The truth is, I had driven up and down the Loch Lomond, Rannoch and Glen Coe roads to Fort William for what seemed like an eternity, listening to the strains of Mike Oldfield and Rick Wakeman, and frequently glancing enviously across at serious-faced West Highland Wayfarers trudging through the rain in Glen Coe, or cowering beneath heavy packs north of Tyndrum, and I felt that I wanted to share the same evidently transcendental experience. So when the chance came to do it and earn money at the same time, I leapt at it – after that two nanoseconds' delay, of course.

With untypical aplomb I rummaged about in search of my backpacking sack, the Trangias and numerous non-essential accessories I always take when backpacking, and then set about the tea bag and biscuit logistics, planning to complete the trek at the end of October 1995, scoot back to base and type it up speedily for publication in the spring of 1996. Sadly, I overlooked the fact that during the time I was there the whole country reverts from daft time to GMT, which left me with an inordinately long walk from Bridge of Orchy to Kinlochleven to do in one day, with the last hours in darkness. Not a problem in normal circumstances, but I was supposed to be working, and I couldn't write about what I couldn't see. So, at the Little Chef in Tyndrum, while consulting a Cajun chicken and chips, Plan B was devised – namely, go home and finish the walk in the spring. As a result, the poor souls at Crianlarich youth hostel who thought they had seen the last of me had to put up with me again, but they were quite brave about it.

More to the point, I got to see the Way in two seasons, and felt I had gained something in doing so. In October, the temperatures had been ideal for backpacking, and the light even better for photography. By May, most of the snow had cleared from the mountains, the rivers and burns were manageable, and the light just as splendid.

Inevitably the time came when it was prudent to look at revising this guide, so the route was walked in its entirety in May 2002: it rained every day!

Remarkably, very little had changed – certainly nothing of the route was different. A larger number of B&Bs along the way were supporting Wayfarers, and the pack-carrying service, which only the stoical will ignore, had come into its own. Not all long-distance walks lend themselves to a pack-carrying service, but this is one that does: it's now called 'Baggage transfer'.

What really stood out was the tremendous sense of camaraderie that developed among walkers travelling on the same day. Over a period of a week, while you're not travelling in one another's pockets you do keep meeting the same people and share experiences. That's good; that's as it should be. Get out of sync, and suddenly you don't know anyone.

Around 17,000 people complete the West Highland Way each year.

That's not bad by any standards. But many set off and don't finish; some don't even complete the first day. The impression I gained is that too many of those who think they can do the Way are ill-prepared, have little experience of day-long walking, day after day, and have equipment that is anything but tried and tested.

Each day's walking should be within your own capability. Use taxis to shunt you about if necessary, but do not attempt to do more than you can comfortably manage. And be prepared to modify your plans.

The revisions for the 2011 edition took place in two parts, not least because on the first visit, in July, the rain was a horizontal waterfall, and not much fun. When I returned in October, things were a little easier weather-wise.

A short description of the route from north to south has been added. The walk is divided into stages (1–7), but these are purely for ease of reference, and are not intended as daily itineraries – however they do correspond with a sensible if slightly demanding 7-day itinerary.

As I prepare a new edition (the 4th, 2016), very little has changed along the route: a few stiles have become gates, a new road bypass around Crianlarich has marginally affected the spur from the Way down into the town, and minor tweaks have appeared to improve the walking. But the beauty of the West Highland Way has diminished not one jot.

Burn of Mar rushes down to Loch Lomond (Stage 2) (photo: Jonathan Williams)

INTRODUCTION

The River Ba (Stage 5)

Now over 35 years old, the West Highland Way (*Slighe na Gàidhealtachd an Iar*) was the first long-distance route to be officially designated in Scotland, established under the Countryside (Scotland) Act, 1967. The idea originated as long ago as the 1930s and 1940s, but it was in the aftermath of the success of the Pennine Way that such embryonic notions began to develop to maturity. The trail was approved for development in September 1974 and was completed and opened on 6 October 1980 by Lord Mansfield, Minister of State at the Scottish Office.

It runs, officially, for 153.2km (95½ miles) from the outskirts of Glasgow to Fort William, and in the process visits an enormously wide variety of landscapes and walking conditions. It is listed by *National Geographic* as one of the world's top 10 best trails, and it was the first European route to become part of the International Appalachian Trail (IAT) (www.iat-sia.org) providing the core of the IAT-Scotland trail from the Mull of Galloway to Cape Wrath. It is now also one of 26 long-distance routes recently designated as Scotland's Great Trails (www.scotlandsgreattrails.org.uk).

Official designations aside, there is a great association between much of the Way and the historical past of Scotland. It crosses three major areas

Fine views over Loch Lomond on the route between Balmaha and Rowardenna (Stage 2) (photo: Jonathan Williams)

of great significance in Scottish history – from the lands of Lennox, through Breadalbane and on to Lochaber. Much of the route pursues ancient drove roads or old military roads built to help in the control of Jacobite clansmen, and the study of these aspects alone is a fascinating and worthwhile preoccupation.

Today's visitors will find that the Way is well-maintained, but is often subject to ongoing sectional improvement, upgrading and repair, such as the adjustment introduced to accommodate the line of the 2014 Crianlarich road by-pass.

FROM THE LOWLANDS TO THE HIGHLANDS

The great pleasure of the Way derives from the many changes in its character as it moves through different geological zones – from Lowland Scotland to the Highlands, and from a pastoral introduction as it moves northwards from Milngavie to the loveliness that is Loch Lomond. Beyond that the route enters the delightful realms of Glen Falloch and Strath Fillan – glens flanked by great mountains that were once cloaked by a mantle of ancient Caledonian pine.

North of Tyndrum, the Way sets about tackling Rannoch Moor, largely on routes formerly used by drovers. As a result, it is well trodden and never in doubt. But it is this section that is more remote from outside help than at any other time along the walk. On a good day the walking is a delight, but, in spite of the comparative ease of the conditions underfoot, poor weather can soon turn delight to

Approaching Conic Hill and Killandan Burn (Stage 2)

disaster. Anyone not bound for the oasis that is the King's House Hotel should think twice, if the weather is especially changeable, before leaving the security of the Bridge of Orchy or Inveroran; there is no shelter worth its name between Bridge of Orchy and Kingshouse.

Touching only briefly on Glen Coe, the Way presses on from Kingshouse, heading for Kinlochleven, the Lairig Mor and Fort William. Parts of the short stretch between Kingshouse and Altnafeadh, alongside the heavy and speeding traffic on the A82, are the least appealing of the whole walk. As Wayfarers approach Altnafeadh they stride along within feet of the traffic for a short distance, and in wet conditions are sure to get a good drenching from spray.

Between Altnafeadh and the end of the Way at Fort William, however, the quality of the walking remains high. On the stretch across to Kinlochleven there is a special sense of isolation amid the eastern slopes and moors of Glencoe. The top of the so-called Devil's Staircase above Altnafeadh is, at 550m (1805ft), the highest point of the entire route. Kinlochleven comes as something of a pleasant surprise, remote by any form of approach, but a great point of access to the wild mountain lands of the Mamores and Glencoe. It was also the first village in the world to have every house connected to electricity, earning it the nickname of 'The Electric Village'.

Forestry plantations cloak the hills on the south side of Glen Nevis, but these have been extensively

17

cleared in recent years, and the continued felling means that occasionally the West Highland Way has to be diverted for a while. Before that, the flight across the southern flanks of the Mamores through the hidden valley of Lairig Mor is excellent walking, and a fitting final stage for an outstanding walk.

The end of the West Highland Way has traditionally been Nevis Bridge at the northern end of Fort William. But in recent years, Nevis Bridge has seen its place usurped by the statue of a seated figure at the southernmost end of Fort William, almost a mile (1.4km) farther on. Logically, there can be no grounds for moving the end so far from Nevis Bridge; it is a fine, if busy, spot, and the author encourages all walkers to call it a day here. You will need to walk into the centre of Fort William, of course, at some point, but that was always the case.

If logic is needed in choosing the end of a trail, then, in this instance, there are a couple of better contenders: the point at which the River Nevis reaches Loch Linnhe, for example; and the town centre green in Fort William. Both of these have the advantage of linking with the ongoing Great Glen Way, and for many Wayfarers the second option is walked anyway.

An alternative finish from the site of Blar a'Chaorainn toll house high above Fort William, invites a speedy conclusion by continuing down the course of the Old Military Road into Fort William via Blarmachfoldach – nearly 5 miles/7.7km of undulating road walking that circumvents the splendours (and, yes, difficulties) of Nevis Forest. As an emergency escape route, this is acceptable, but it is a poor way to conclude such a fine walk.

HOW HARD AND HOW REMOTE?

The West Highland Way is neither easy nor outrageously demanding. Inclement weather can certainly

The view across Loch Lomond from near Cailness (photo: Jonathan Williams)

A last look at Lairig Mor (Stage 7)

raise the stakes a few notches, but neither is it the ideal route on which to embark on your first experience of long-distance walking. Fit, healthy and experienced walkers accustomed to long days on the hills will encounter no difficulty in tackling the West Highland Way. For anyone else, it would be foolish even to think about setting off without having previously done a deal of rough walking – ideally with a pack heavier than might be required for day use, even if intending to use the West Highland Way pack-carrying services.

Because it makes use of those old drove roads and military roads, which in turn have been fairly faithfully followed by 20th-century roads and railway links, the resulting route is never far from help, although it can seem to be on a bad day. Only on the crossing of Rannoch Moor and passing through Lairig Mor beyond and above Kinlochleven is there any real sense of isolation.

Yet the Way's proximity to such modern trappings of civilisation rarely impinges on the pleasure gained from the walk. Yes, there are moments when the sound of traffic intrudes and the Way comes perilously close to it; and, yes, there are times when the traffic seems always in view, somewhere. But that must be set against a walk of great quality and distinction that passes through a landscape second to none. Often all it takes to evade these 'problems' is a convenient boulder or sheltered hollow, and you could be a million miles from anywhere.

PLANNING YOUR TRIP

Light and dark – the moods of the Lairig Mor (Stage 7)

SUGGESTED ITINERARIES

The Trek Planner at the front of this guide shows the distance between each of the principal halts along the Way, and what facilities are available at those locations. Using this, you should be able construct a walk to suit you, but beware not to be over-ambitious in planning a day's walk.

The Way is described in seven stages in this guide, and the table below offers three alternative itineraries involving overnight stops at places where accommodation and other facilities are available.

However, you must plan your daily walk according to your own strengths and abilities.

Doing the walk in six days is demanding and allows no rest (or easy) days. Seven or eight days is much more comfortable, especially if you have limited experience of distance walking. You can make nine days of it by breaking the Drymen to Rowardennan section at Balmaha, allowing time to visit Inchcailloch. Your walk must become what you want it to be – not a forced march. If you can, take your time and use it as a gateway to exploration of the countryside that lies to either side of it.

Start	Finish	Distance
6-day schedule		
Milngavie	Drymen	12½ miles (20km)
Drymen	Rowardennan	15 miles (24km)
Rowardennan	Crianlarich	20 miles (32.5km)
Crianlarich	Inveroran	15¾ miles (25km)
Inveroran	Kinlochleven	18½ miles (29.5km)
Kinlochleven	Fort William	13¾ miles (22km)
8-day schedule		
Milngavie	Drymen	12½ miles (20km)
Drymen	Rowardennan	15 miles (24km)
Rowardennan	Inverarnan	13¾ miles (22km)
Inverarnan	Crianlarich	6¾ miles (11km)
Crianlarich	Bridge of Orchy	13 miles (21km)
Bridge of Orchy	Kingshouse	12¼ miles (19.5km)
Kingshouse	Kinlochleven	8¾ miles (14km)
Kinlochleven	Fort William	13¾ miles (22km)
9-day schedule		
Milngavie	Drymen	12½ miles (20km)
Drymen	Balmaha	7½ miles (12km)
Balmaha	Rowardennan	7½ miles (12km)
Rowardennan	Inverarnan	13¾ miles (22km)
Inverarnan	Crianlarich	6¾ miles (11km)
Crianlarich	Bridge of Orchy	13 miles (21km)
Bridge of Orchy	Kingshouse	12¼ miles (19.5km)
Kingshouse	Kinlochleven	8¾ miles (14km)
Kinlochleven	Fort William	13¾ miles (22km)

WHEN TO GO

Over the many years that I have been backpacking in Scotland I have, at various times, encountered weather that has grilled my ears to an acute degree of tenderness and, at others, drenched me so thoroughly that it would have been simpler, but infinitely more embarrassing, to walk with nothing on at all! Both extremes should be expected and catered for by anyone contemplating the West Highland Way. Only those who don't think in terms of such weather conditions are likely to find themselves facing uncomfortable and (at the extreme) potentially dangerous conditions.

In Scotland, weather statistics are meaningless, made even more pointless by the fact that many walkers on the West Highland Way simply cannot sit at home until the weather looks like settling for a week or so and then zoom to Glasgow to begin the walk. The reality is that you get whatever weather you get, and you have to be able to cope with it. There is a saying – something of a hackneyed cliché now – that there is no such thing as bad weather, just inadequate clothing. There is a lot of truth in this – so if you expect cold, wet and windy weather, and prepare for it, then anything else is a bonus. Approach the West Highland Way in this frame of mind – equipped to cope with the worst – and then when you find beautiful days of perfect walking weather you'll come to believe that the sun really does shine on the righteous.

One of the least expected consequences of bad weather is the effect it can have on even the tiniest burns (streams), turning them into raging torrents that can prove difficult to cross. To a large extent this has been anticipated by the managing authorities for the Way, and footbridges have been installed wherever this is likely to occur, but there is always at least one exception that seems set on proving the rule. Unless time is genuinely of the essence, the wisest way of dealing with these extreme conditions is to retreat and sit them out in safety and comfort for a while. They seldom last long and, with the exception of misty conditions and forecast bouts of prolonged bad weather, usually clear up in a brief period of time.

You have little freedom over when you tackle the Way, but, if you do, there are certain times to be avoided, sometimes for less obvious reasons than the (limited) congestion you can expect during the main tourist months of July and August. It's a good idea, for example, to avoid starting at weekends: if you can start midweek, do so.

While working on the first edition of this book I walked the Way in October and late May, and on both occasions weather conditions were ideal. May and June, and September and October, are most likely to offer the best and most settled weather (although foul weather is still possible). But there are two periods to avoid during these months if possible: the first week of May sees motorcycle trials being held on sections of the Way between Bridge of Orchy and Fort William. Earlier in the year you may find route diversions to take account of lambing, while later in the year there is the minor inconvenience of deer stalking and rather larger inconvenience of the midge season.

Deer stalking and lambing
Both deer stalking and lambing play a vital part in the economic life of the Highlands.

Deer populations in the highlands are part of the magnificent wildlife heritage, but deer stalking is also a much valued sporting activity. Many people see the culling of deer – particularly when it forms part of the sporting process – as wrong, but it should be remembered that because the deer have no natural enemies their culling is considered necessary to maintain a healthy population and to reduce their impact on the countryside.

Stalking usually takes place between mid August and mid October, but is unlikely to affect walkers sticking to the West Highland Way. Only when you plan to branch off from the Way should you seek permission locally. Walkers who show proper consideration for the interests of those engaged in the management of the deer populations and the estates will find most of them accommodating and helpful in suggesting alternative routes that will not interfere with their activities. You can find more information about deer stalking on www.outdooraccess-scotland.com.

Lambing is also a sensitive time for many of the hill farmers. The busiest time runs from mid March to May, and walkers should pay particular attention to the need to avoid disturbing, and possibly distressing, pregnant ewes at this time. As elsewhere, do not pick up lambs that appear to have been abandoned. If possible, report the fact to the nearest farm – you will be doing much more good that way, and fostering good relations between walkers and the farming communities of Scotland.

Midges and ticks
One of the purgatorial experiences of walking in Scotland is the ubiquitous midge, a tiny biting insect that seems to regard humans as little more than an al fresco dining experience on legs. Like wolves, they hunt in packs, but in greater numbers, and to be surrounded by a cloud of these vicious beasties all clamouring for a taste of your fleshier parts is not a pleasant event. They seem to be at the worst from the end of May onwards, and have allies in the form of horse flies (known as clegs) and sheep ticks.

There are a few proprietary creams, lotions and sprays that have some deterrent effect, and in recent times creams have been based on bog myrtle (*Myrica gale*) – a traditional highland remedy for midges in particular. Oil of lavender also seems to have a beneficial effect for a while, but needs to be constantly reapplied, leaving you smelling rather pungent by the end of the day. One proprietary solution, allegedly used by our stalwart marines, is Avon's 'Skin so Soft', which does work quite effectively.

Thankfully, midges cannot take to the air in even light breezes, making this little gem of knowledge important to anyone faced with pitching a tent; better the flapping sides of a tent to contend with than furiously flapping arms inside it as you do battle with the insects all night.

Ticks are likely to be present during the warmer months, especially where bracken is adjacent to the path. Ticks may carry Lyme disease so it is advisable to wear long trousers when walking through any form of vegetation. At the end of the day's walking, check yourself to see if any have attached themselves. This is equally important if you are walking with a dog, on which ticks are much harder to find. They can be removed by taking a pair of tweezers and grasping

them firmly where they are attached to the skin. Then gently twist anti-clockwise until the tick is free. Take care to remove the whole tick and not leave part of its body attached. If you do get tick bites and feel unwell, seek medical assistance. More information is available at www.lymediseaseaction.org.uk/about-lyme/faq.

GETTING THERE AND BACK

Long-distance rail services from London and intermediate stations operate to Glasgow and to Edinburgh by Virgin Trains East Coast and West Coast services. Rail services operate from Glasgow Central, Glasgow Queen Street and Edinburgh Waverley direct to Milngavie.

Milngavie

From Glasgow, Milngavie is also served by local bus (Buchanan Street

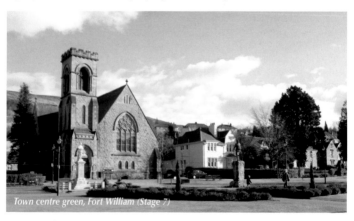

Town centre green, Fort William (Stage 7)

bus station). The train service is the more convenient option for access to the West Highland Way, with a more frequent service, twice an hour for most of the day, terminating in Milngavie, so you can't miss your stop. The official start of the Way, in the Douglas Street precinct, is a few minutes' walk from the station.

Fort William

Fort William is served by both long-distance coach services to and from the north, east and south, and trains, on the West Highland Line, to Glasgow. There is no train service between Fort William and Inverness. Details of coach services can be found at www.citylink.co.uk and train services at www.scotrail.co.uk. Coaches and trains go to and from the northern end of the town centre.

TRANSPORT ALONG THE ROUTE

With few exceptions, the West Highland Way is seldom far from a road or a railway, so it is feasible to walk it in short sections using public transport. The services, however, are not frequent. If you are thinking of trying this option make sure you get up-to-date timetables from the information centres in Glasgow, Milngavie or Fort William, or bus and rail stations (see Appendix A).

Details of the Waterbus services across Loch Lomond, which allow walkers the opportunity to head

for accommodation and facilities on the west shore, are also given in Appendix A.

In case you were thinking of using your bike along the Way, it is worth noting that although it does make use of many old roads, it is a route designated for walkers. Many parts of the route are possible on suitable bikes, but as a whole it is not for cyclists.

FIRST NIGHTS AND LAST NIGHTS

Milngavie

Milngavie (www.milngavieonline. com) is very much a commuter town and a popular retirement location with a high proportion of elderly; its renown appears to rest entirely on its place in the walking world as the starting point of the West Highland Way. The pedestrianised town centre, known as 'Milngavie Precinct' is based around the original village centre, which also features a number of pubs serving bar meals, and a couple of hotels.

Fort William

The lochside town of Fort William (www.visitfortwilliam.co.uk) has played a significant part in the political history of Scotland, and the wider area has many ancient castle ruins that are worth visiting. The town itself has everything a tired walker

Camping beside the Abhainn Shira (Stage 5)

might need, from comfy hotel beds to a range of well-priced eateries and pubs, a supermarket, outdoor and general retail shops. It is a splendid setting, on the shores of Loch Linnhe and at the foot of Ben Nevis, Britain's highest mountain.

ACCOMMODATION EN ROUTE

For a walk that spends a deal of its time away from civilisation, the Way is well supported with accommodation throughout its entire length. But don't take it for granted; book ahead. A day at a time may suffice at quiet times of the year but in the main tourist season there is pressure on all the accommodation along the Way. In the quieter months some closes down altogether.

The range of accommodation is quite remarkable. In addition to the B&Bs, guest houses, hotels and camping sites that you would expect, the Way boasts three good youth hostels ideally placed for Wayfarers, plus a number of bothies, 'wigwam' shelters (basic wooden structures without facilities – although there are always facilities nearby), bunkhouses and private hostels. There are even small woodland campsites set within the boundaries of the Loch Lomond Park, specifically created with walkers in mind. The Waterbus service across Loch Lomond (see Appendix A) enables walkers to take advantage of accommodation on the western shore and along the A82.

Appendix B contains a basic listing of current accommodation provision, and an up-to-date version of it appears on the Cicerone website (www.cicerone.co.uk/857/accommodation). There are also up-to-date accommodation listings on the internet, such as on www.walkinginscotland.org and www.west-highland-way.co.uk. In addition, consult the appropriate tourist boards (see Appendix A) for information, as the situation is changing all the time.

FACILITIES EN ROUTE

The trek planner details the facilities along the route, but the West Highland Way spends a good deal of time away from civilisation where facilities are non-existent. Nor should it be expected that remote villages are well endowed with shops and cafés that are necessarily open when you arrive, if they exist at all. Moreover, because local transport tends to serve the needs of local people it cannot be relied on to facilitate a quick trip to a shop or large town.

There are few sections of the walk where it is possible to get lunch during the day, so it is vital that you start each day well prepared and stocked. Have a good breakfast; carry plenty of liquid and daytime food, and make the most of an evening meal.

PACK-CARRYING SERVICES

The proximity of the West Highland Way to major highways has seen a new service evolve – that of pack carrying. A number of small companies and taxi firms offer to carry your heavy pack from one location to another on a daily or occasional basis. If you have difficulty carrying heavy loads, and would appreciate the benefits of doing the Way with a day sack, perhaps the pack-carrying service is the thing to use. Details are included in Appendix A.

CASH MANAGEMENT

With few opportunities along the Way to get hold of cash, it becomes vitally important to estimate your money requirements in advance; you cannot rely on all accommodation providers accepting credit and debit card payments. Along the Way you can get cash at the following places:
- Milngavie (banks and ATM machines)
- Drymen (Royal Bank of Scotland and ATMs)
- Crianlarich (cashpoint in Crianlarich Store and post office)
- Tyndrum (cashpoint in the Green Welly Stop)
- Kinlochleven (Royal Bank of Scotland, Thursday only)
- Fort William (banks and ATMs)

A cheque book and banker's card can usually be used to get cash from post offices, and there are post offices in Ardlui, Crianlarich and Tyndrum (in addition to the places where there are banks).

Heading for Blar a'Chaorainn (Stage 7)

PREPARATION AND WHAT TO TAKE

Getting yourself into condition is neither an arduous nor an unpleasant process, and every walk done in preparation will make the experience and enjoyment of the Way all the better.

Nor does conditioning extend only to your physical condition. It is vitally important, for example, to avoid wearing boots that are not 'broken in' or clothing that has not had the chance to lose its newness. Comfort on a long walk can be critically important; discomfort can be painful if allowed to go on too long. If you feel blisters coming on, or your boots start rubbing around the ankles, make sure you attend to the problem sooner rather than later.

What to take

All walkers have their own preferences in the matter of equipment and clothing. When extending day-walking into multiple-day walking much the same general items are needed, with the emphasis on being able to stay warm, dry (as much as possible) and comfortable in all weather conditions.

The following list may be a useful reminder:

- rucksack (comfortable, well padded, appropriate to backpacking rather than day-walking, and preferably already used by you, if only on trial walks)
- boots
- socks (spare socks and more spare socks)
- trousers (and shorts if you wish but not shorts alone)

- underclothes
- shirt
- mid-wear (e.g. pullover) and spare
- wind- and waterproof jacket and over-trousers
- hat
- gloves
- maps
- compass
- torch (with spare battery and bulbs)
- whistle
- first aid kit including blister pads
- survival bag or space blanket
- food and drink
- insect repellent
- washing tackle, including half a roll of toilet tissue (for emergencies)
- small hand towel
- and, if you're using a GPS, then don't forget to carry spare batteries.

Campers will also need such additional weighty items as tent, sleeping bag, sleeping mat, and cooking equipment and utensils. Pedal-bin liners have a number of useful purposes – keeping wet clothes separate from dry in the sack; containing burst packets of food and rubbish until a suitable disposal point can be reached; and insulating dry socks from wet boots when walking.

Take a notebook and keep a personal record of your experiences, or a paperback book to read.

Taking your dog

Attempting the West Highland Way and taking a dog with you is not really practical. There are few accommodation providers who accept dogs, and this directs you towards camping and/or wigwam experiences. Moreover, to complete the route in fewer than 10 days requires a very tough and long-walk experienced pooch. There are also few veterinary services along the Way. But if the route is done piecemeal, a day

A fine late afternoon at Loch Lomond on the route between Balmaha and Rowardennan (Stage 2) (photo: Jonathan Williams)

Beinn Odhar from the watershed north of Tyndrum (Section 4)

or two at a time, and you do decide to take your dog, then there are certain considerations to take into account.

Keep your dog under proper control. You can do this by:

- never letting it worry or attack livestock
- never taking it into a field where there are calves or lambs
- keeping it on a short lead or under close control in fields where there are farm animals
- keeping calm if cattle react aggressively and move towards you, letting the dog go and taking the shortest, safest route out of the field
- keeping it on a short lead or under close control during the bird breeding season (usually April to July) in areas such as moorland, forests, grassland, loch shores and the seashore
- picking up and removing any faeces if your dog defecates in a public open place.

PLANNING DAY BY DAY

Black Rock Cottage, Glencoe
(Stage 5)

USING THIS GUIDE

The guide offers a full step-by-step description of the West Highland Way from south to north. Each stage description is also followed by a summary of the route in reverse for those who like to go against the flow. For ease of reference, the route is divided into seven stages, although these are not necessarily to be taken as day-stages – that is for you to decide (see 'Suggested itineraries', above), but please be sure not to overstretch yourself. The West Highland Way is immensely pleasurable, but not when you are weary. Keep it simple; keep it within your capability.

Each stage starts with some key information (distance, ascent, walking time) and an overview to give you a feel of the terrain and the route. There then follows a route description that highlights in bold key places and features that appear on the 1:100K route maps which accompany the description, and also provides additional information on sites of particular interest, with historical, archaeological, sociological and other significance. In addition, the map booklet included at the back of this guide shows the full route of the West Highland Way on 1:25,000 OS mapping.

The route summary table and trek planner at the front of the guide should help you get an overview of the whole route and plan your own itinerary along it, taking account of

Entering Strath Blane at Arlehaven (Stage 1)

the facilities available. Finally, appendices provide some useful organisations' contact details (Appendix A), details of accommodation along the route (Appendix B), and a list of both essential and supplementary reading, some or all of which will enhance your experience of the walk (Appendix C).

Distances, ascent and descent

To ensure accuracy when giving distances, ascent and descent in the guide, detailed measurements were made using computerised mapping. Because of this, figures for distances given in the guide may differ slightly from the official distances, and, for that matter, data given in earlier editions of this guide; any such discrepancy, however, is unlikely to

be significant. All figures have been rounded up or down.

Walking times

How long it might take to walk 10 miles with a pack varies from individual to individual. Naismith's Rule (1 hour per 3 miles, plus 1 hour for each 2000 feet of ascent) is purely a guide and needs adjustment to suit each walker's personal abilities; not everyone can maintain Naismith's targets over an extended day, such as the section from Rowardennan to Crianlarich.

For this reason, the walking times given are already an adjustment of Naismith's Rule based on the author's own experience; they are intended just to give an idea of how long you may need to be walking. Of course, the times given make no allowance for any kind of stopping, photographic, refreshment or otherwise.

Should you want to explore more widely, perhaps while taking a day off, Ordnance Survey also covers the West Highland Way on a number of 1:25,000 maps:
- Explorer 342 (Glasgow);
- Explorer 347 (Loch Lomond South);
- Explorer 348 (Campsie Fells);
- Explorer 364 (Loch Lomond North);
- Explorer 377 (Loch Etive and Glen Orchy);
- Explorer 384 (Glen Coe and Glen Etive) and
- Explorer 392 (Ben Nevis and Fort William).

Harvey Maps produce a map for the Way at a scale of 1:40,000, which comes folded in a plastic wallet and arranged in panels so that at any one time you only have open the part you need.

The whole of the West Highland Way is also available for the SatMap Active 10/12 GPS device (www. satmap.co.uk), which provides complete and accurate coverage of progress along the Way using satellite technology.

Other mobile mapping solutions are available from Garmin, Viewranger, the Ordnance Survey themselves, and others.

WAYMARKING

The West Highland Way has been sensitively and sensibly waymarked. The emblem is simply a white thistle within a hexagon on a post, and there are very few superfluous waymarks. Where the line of the route is abundantly clear, as for example across Rannoch Moor, there is no waymarking at all, which is as it should be. Those responsible for waymarking should be commended.

Even with this unobtrusive level of waymarking, it is perfectly feasible to travel the route without real fear of getting lost, and it could be argued that the route description in this guide does no more than put flesh on what would be the very bare bones of the waymarks. In addition, it aims to provide a measure of reassurance and guidance to those who need it, and a wealth of background information for those who want to take in the landscape and the culture through which the Way passes.

EMERGENCIES

The police, fire service, ambulance or mountain rescue can be reached in an emergency by dialling 999 or 112. There are numerous mountain rescue teams operating in the regions covered by the West Highland Way; the appropriate one can be contacted on the above emergency numbers:
- Arrochar MRT – www.arrocharmrt.org.uk

Ascending from the Bridge of Orchy to Màm Carraigh (Stage 4)

- Glencoe MRT – www.glencoe
  mountainrescue.org.uk
- Killin MRT – killin.mountain
  rescuescotland.org
- Lochaber MRT – www.lochaber
  mrt.co.uk
- Lomond MRT – www.lomondmrt.
  org.uk
- Ochils MRT – www.omrt.org.uk

WEATHER FORECASTS

Britain is meteorologically sandwiched between moist maritime air and dry continental air – a combination that creates large temperature variations and atmospheric instability. As a result, many (and sometimes all) weather variations can be experienced in just one day. That said, there are often pro-longed periods of stable weather that make recreational walking an utter joy.

Weather forecasting is much improved in recent years, with the best forecasts on a day-to-day basis being provided by regional television channels.

The Met Office have a download-able weather app (www.metoffice. gov.uk) in a new format introduced in 2016. It is available from iPhone's App Store (itunes.apple.com) and Android's Google Play Store (play. google.com/store/apps). The app is designed to work on iOS 8 and above, and Android 4.1 and above.

'Weather Live' is arguably the best of the non-Met Office apps, also available for iPhones and Androids, although there are plenty of others.

The Mountain Weather UK App consolidates weather and avalanche forecasts for all UK mountain areas in a single app.

PHONES AND INTERNET

Wi-Fi internet access is increasingly available in cafés, pubs and hotels throughout Scotland, but it is by no means universally available, and may not always be available in B&Bs or youth hostels.

Mobile phone signals are restricted in coverage and often erratic – especially away from main urban centres. 2G coverage is reasonably wide-spread along the West Highland Way; 3G rather less so, and 4G mainly around Glasgow and Fort William. But it is improving at an impressive rate, and there are often seemingly bizarre and unexpected locations where reception is good – usually from a link with some distant mast.

You can check your own service provider's coverage on their website, but the reality is that you will not have a signal or connection along many of the open and remote stretches of the Way.

ALL ABOUT THE HIGHLANDS

Along the banks of Loch Lomond (Stage 2)

GEOGRAPHY

The Highlands region is sparsely populated, much less so than of old. Before the 19th century, the Highlands sustained a much larger population, but that was gradually reduced by a combination of factors: the outlawing of the traditional Highland way of life following the Jacobite uprising of 1745; the forced displacements of the so-called Highland Clearances during the 18th and 19th centuries, and the migrations in search of employment inspired by the Industrial Revolution between about 1760 and 1840.

The West Highland Way links two main urban centres – Milngavie on the outskirts of Glasgow, and Fort William in Lochaber, with only minor settlements in between – Crianlarich, Tyndrum and Kinlochleven. The route uses ancient roads – notably drovers' routes, military roads and old coaching routes.

The first stage of the walk, usually done south to north, is across the landscape of the Central Lowlands (see 'Geology' below), predominantly featuring the gentle-shaped, low-lying characteristics of woodland and farmland. Once Loch Lomond is reached, the nature of the landscape changes to one very much influenced by the geology of the Highlands and Islands region, and produces a dramatic, inspirational and occasionally threatening aura of mountains and valleys. Scotland, as a whole, has the most mountainous terrain in the whole of Britain, and a decent slice of it is encountered along the West Highland Way.

GEOLOGY

The geology of Scotland is surprisingly varied for a country of its size, with numerous differing geological features. Initial impressions are that this is simply a land of high volcanic mountains, and that is what is most noticeable about the West Highland Way.

The bigger picture reveals three main geographical sub-divisions: the 'Highlands and Islands' – a diverse area to the north and west of the Highland Boundary Fault; the 'Central Lowlands' – a rift valley mainly comprising Palaeozoic formations; and the 'Southern Uplands', which lie south of the Southern Uplands Fault and are composed of Silurian deposits.

The Southern Uplands can be ignored so far as the West Highland Way is concerned. But that Highland Boundary Fault, which runs from the Isle of Arran to Stonehaven on the east coast, becomes a very evident and pronounced feature on only the second day of the walk, marked by the line of Conic Hill above Loch Lomond. At one point, mentioned in the text, you can clearly see the distinction between the geology to the north of the fault line and that to the south.

The Highlands (we can forget the 'Islands') are generally mountainous and bisected by the Great Glen Fault. Some of the highest elevations in the British Isles are found here, including Ben Nevis, the highest peak at 1345m

Dumgoyne, a distinctive summit at the edge of the Campsie Fells (Stage 1)

37

(4413ft). The Great Glen fault runs northwards from Fort William, so the West Highland Way is clearly sandwiched between two important geological features. The Highlands region largely comprises ancient rocks, from Cambrian and Precambrian times, uplifted to form a mountain chain, and interspersed with igneous intrusions of more recent age.

PLANTS AND WILDLIFE

The fauna of Scotland is typical of northwest Europe, although many large mammals were hunted to extinction in historic times. Even so, there are over 60 species of wild mammals, including the wild cat – 'at-risk' (possibly from inter-breeding with domestic cats). Historically, much of Scotland was covered by the great Caledonian Forest, but this has been reduced by people, sheep and deer to just one per cent of its greatest extent (writer George Monbiot, in *Feral*). There are still a few places where these trees still grow: the youngest more than 150 years old; the oldest dating from the time of Culloden (1746). Along the West Highland Way, however, there is little to see save a few petrified root balls in Glen Falloch.

Red deer are everywhere and increasingly proving to be a problem that frustrates regeneration of trees in particular. There are those who think that the solution to what they see as the deer problem is the reintroduction of wolves. It hasn't happened yet.

Wayfarers will have many opportunities to see moorland birds, including the black and red grouse. The golden eagle is widespread, while white-tailed eagles roam widely (although rarely far from the sea), and ospreys, which recently re-colonised

Strath Blane landscape (Stage 1)

parts of the Highlands, may be seen on passage. The Scottish crossbill is the only endemic vertebrate species in the UK, although these tend to be found further east than the West Highland Way.

Although the Scottish thistle is the emblem of the West Highland Way, they are not widespread along the route. Heather and ling, however, grow in abundance, and are colourful additions to seasonal visits.

HISTORY AND CULTURE

Anyone walking the West Highland Way is taking a walk through a history liberally endowed with scenes of massacre, betrayal, lawlessness and military action, but the walk itself is a part of history, part of the process of liberalising the countryside for the benefit of those seeking to escape the gloomy confines of Britain's towns and cities. This 'fight back' against landowners' gamekeepers was started in Lancashire in the late 19th century, and continued 40 years later in the Peak District. North of the border, the tradition of weekend escapes to the mountains of the Highlands saw the roots of the West Highland Way firmly planted as long ago as the 1930s.

Between the 15th and 20th centuries, the Highland region differed from the Lowlands most significantly in terms of its language. In Scottish Gaelic, the region is known as the Gàidhealtachd, denoting the traditional Gaelic-speaking part of Scotland.

In the aftermath of the Jacobite uprisings (1715 and 1745), the British government enacted laws designed to destroy the clan system, including a ban on the wearing of tartan. Most of the legislation was repealed towards the end of the 18th century and led to a restoration of Highland culture that saw tartan adopted for Highland regiments in the British Army. For 'ordinary' people, however, tartan had been abandoned. But in the 1820s, tartan and the kilt were adopted by members of the social elite, which aroused an international craze for tartan, and for idealising a romanticised Highlands, that was set off by the Ossian cycle of epic poems by the Scottish poet James Macpherson from 1760, and further popularised by the works of Walter Scott, whose 'staging' of the visit of King George IV to Scotland in 1822 and the king's wearing of tartan resulted in a massive upsurge in demand for kilts and tartans. This 'Highlandistic trend', by which all of Scotland was identified with the culture of the Highlands, was cemented by Queen Victoria's interest in the country, and her adoption of Balmoral as a major royal retreat.

FOOD AND DRINK

The popular imagery of Scottish food is that of haggis and porridge. The latter is a dish made with oatmeal and water and cooked with a small amount of salt, though many people substitute milk for water, and leave out the salt.

The description of haggis is not instantly appealing, but it has an excellent texture and savoury flavour being made from the heart, liver and lungs of a sheep minced with onion, oatmeal, suet and salt and traditionally encased in an animal's stomach (but increasingly these days in an artificial casing). You can find haggis served widely, usually with tatties (potatoes) and neeps (turnip). Fill your belly with that, and wash it down with a glass of whisky, and you won't want for much more.

You may also come across cold smoked herring on your Wayfarings: 'kippers', served for breakfast, are a typically British food popular throughout Scotland. Black pudding (*marag dubh*), too, declared in 2016 to be the new superfood, and of such national importance that the black pudding produced in Stornoway in the Outer Hebrides has been awarded special protected status. The puddings are made from beef suet, oatmeal, onion, blood from sheep, cows or pigs and seasoning.

Those with a sweet tooth should look out for:

- cranachan – made from raspberries, whipped cream, honey and toasted oats, sometimes with a dram of whisky added
- tablet – a traditional Scottish sweet made from sugar, condensed milk and butter, often flavoured with vanilla
- shortbread – a luxurious biscuit made with a generous amount of butter
- clootie dumpling – a rich fruit pudding made with flour, breadcrumbs, dried fruit, suet, sugar, spice, milk and golden syrup, served with cream and a dram of whisky

Of course, the drink most synonymous with Scotland is whisky, simply called Scotch – a malt whisky or grain whisky made in a manner specified by law. Malt whisky is produced from water and malted barley at a single distillery; Grain whisky likewise, but it may include whole grains or malted or unmalted cereals. These distinctions aside, the simplistic notion of Scottish whisky is that it is either a single malt or a blended whisky (which may blend whiskies from more than one distillery). Both are excellent, and there are a great many distilleries producing whisky, popularly known as *uisce beatha* – the water of life.

THE WEST HIGHLAND WAY

Descending from the Tyndrum watershed (Stage 4)

STAGE 1
Milngavie to Drymen

Start	Centre of Milngavie (NS 554 745)
Finish	Junction of B858 and A809, Drymen (NS 481 888)
Distance	12½ miles (20km) – including short walk to the centre of Drymen
Total ascent	835ft (255m)
Total descent	845ft (257m)
Walking time	5½–6hrs
Terrain	A comparatively easy start to the Way, largely on good paths, tracks and lanes with no significant climbing; woodland, open pasture; railway trackbed.
Accommodation	Milngavie, Easter Drumquhassle, Drymen

The first stretch of the West Highland Way speeds walkers away from the conurbation of Glasgow and soon has them enjoying the fertile, pastoral landscapes through which the Way threads a route. There is constantly changing scenery and variable conditions underfoot – from quiet country lanes to farmland and even the trackbed of an old railway, which can be quite glutinous after rain. The whole impression, however, is one of a calm and relaxing introduction to the rigours (such as they are) that lie ahead.

Strong walkers will make it to Balmaha and Loch Lomond, or further, in one day. But the West Highland Way is not a route for rushing; time should be built in to take on board the many varied delights, and a planned overnight stay at or near Drymen gives a first day with which to be satisfied before heading for the watershed between lowland and highland Scotland at the southern edge of the Lomond basin.

There are few opportunities to buy refreshments along the way, so self-sufficiency needs to be the order of the day – even if you do ultimately succumb to the temptation of the occasional pub.

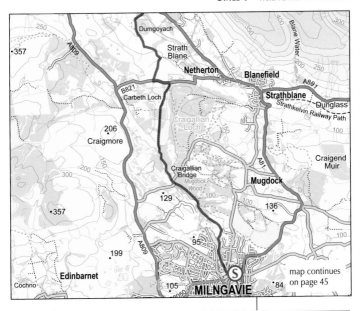

map continues
on page 45

MILNGAVIE

Perhaps the most significant feature of Milngavie – a charming Glasgow sub-
urb and commuter town with a proud independence – that Wayfarers need
to be aware of is that its name is pronounced (approximately) 'Mull-guy'.
Without this knowledge you may never reach the start of the walk. Quite
where the name comes from is obscure. Some suggest it may have been
from Meall na Gaoithe ('the hill of the wind'), or from muileann-gaoithe ('a
windmill'). There would certainly have been a number of mills here in times
gone by, including a paper mill and a cotton mill, so the connection is a
plausible one.

Tramcars from Glasgow once swayed their way to Milngavie; now their
place has been taken by a modern railway, and during the summer months
there's a distinct impression that this is a charter service for Wayfarers.

The land surrounding Milngavie historically comprised several estates
with tenant farms, but many stone-built villas and semi-detached houses

43

were constructed, notably along Station Road to the east of the town centre and around Tannoch Loch, for wealthy Victorian citizens once commuting to Glasgow was made possible by the opening of the railway in 1863. Many of the extant properties show Scottish cottage, Scottish Baronial, Classical architecture and Gothic influences, which goes some way to explaining why this is part of a conservation area of historical significance. Today there are few remains of the pre-Victorian village other than the Corbie Ha' meeting hall, Cross Keys public house (now called Garvie & Co) and the Gavin's Mill water mill on the Allander Water along with Barloch House and Barloch Farm.

Robert McLellan OBE (1907–1985), the playwright, poet and writer of short fiction (principally in the Scots language), grew up in the town where his father founded and ran the local Allander Press, which had premises in the Black Bull Yard in the early 20th century.

Liberal Democrat politician Jo Swinson was born and brought up in Milngavie, and attended the local Douglas Academy. She was Parliamentary Under Secretary of State for employment relations, consumer and postal affairs in the 2010 Coalition, but lost her seat in the 2015 General Election.

The route begins with some (inconsequential) controversy about the exact start of the West Highland Way; immediately adjacent to the railway station is a large board announcing the start of the Way, while local opinion considers that the Way begins at a neat granite obelisk – unveiled by a local councillor in 1992 – in the centre of town. The distinction is immaterial, since walkers who come by train start from the station anyway, just as everyone did before the obelisk was built, while those who come by any other means of public or private transport still have to walk to the obelisk, which stands in the middle of a neat pedestrianised oasis.

From the station go left and through an underpass to ascend steps into Station Road, and follow waymarks and signs for the West Highland Way. Keep ahead through a pedestrian precinct, passing the Cross Keys Inn to reach the obelisk.

At the obelisk, the start of the Way is conspicuously waymarked and heads down a ramped walkway to effect

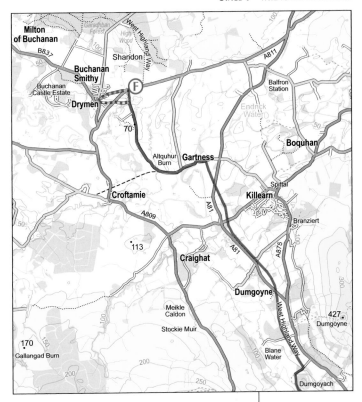

a somewhat ignominious start through a shopping service area. Cross a car park, trending right and ignoring the tempting bridge on the left. Walk out to meet a road, then turn left on a tarmac path beside a burn. The Way soon goes under a road and enters a tree-lined and acoustically screened cutting with steep, sloping banks that once accommodated a small railway serving a paper mill on Allander Water.

Within minutes the sound of a modestly busy town is left well behind, as the trackbed shepherds walkers on to the rear of Milngavie library and a leisure centre. Quite soon the Way leaves the railway route, going left into woodland to reach a large pond. Here, go right and right again a few strides later to court Allander Water through pleasant woodland, a brief riparian ramble in the company of dippers and grey wagtails.

Ignore the bridge that spans Allander Water and press on beside the burn into the more open expanse of Allander Park. These early stages of the walk are inevitably dogged by the trappings of 'civilisation', but are quite agreeable in spite of the unglamorous aspect of warehouses on the opposite side of the burn and the noise of aircraft heading for Glasgow airport.

The embryonic panorama from the ridge captures the suburbs of Glasgow and the Kirkpatrick Hills, and quietly sets the tone for what lies ahead.

Thankfully, all this is short-lived, as a waymarked path leads away from the burn to rise across the lush upper part of the park, which proves to be a pleasantly untidy spread of rough moorland supporting a range of trees, bracken, gorse and tussock grass. A short haul climbs to the first of many vantage points that the Way has in store – a ridge formed from ancient lavas. ◄

From the high point, the Way goes ahead and then left, through more woodland comprised of birch, oak, beech, rowan and gorse. Ignore a branching path on

Making a start in Mugdock Country Park

the right, and later turnings at a crosspath, always keeping ahead to enter Mugdock Country Park – a Sensitive Wildlife Area.

Gifted in 1980 to the people of Glasgow, Mugdock Wood and the surrounding area of established mixed woodland now forms the **Mugdock Country Park**, which is an important ecological site with notable species of flowers, an oak woodland and an attractive loch. The park includes the remains of the 14th-century Mugdock Castle, stronghold of the Grahams of Montrose, and the ruins of the 19th-century Craigend Castle, a Gothic Revival mansion. The park has a moot hill and gallowhill – historical reminders of the baronial feudal right held by lairds and described in full as 'pit and gallows, sake and soke, toll, team, and infangthief'.

On entering the country park, cross a culverted stream and then press on through attractive woodland along the former drive to Craigallian House, flanked on the left by Allander Water. Already the urbanity of Milngavie is forgotten and the route is one of pleasurable woodland walking where birdsong invariably helps you on your way.

Ignore a tempting deviation to Mugdock Castle, and keep on instead to leave **Mugdock Wood** at a lane. Go left, downhill, for a short distance, and then leave the lane on the right to enter an area managed by the Loch Lomond Countryside Park Ranger Service.

As you pass through Mugdock, you're striding through the old Barony of Mugdock, centred on **Mugdock Castle**, the principal seat of the chief of the Graham clan, whose members have played an important part in Scottish history. The lands of Mugdock were a property of the Grahams from the mid-13th century, when David de Graham bought them from the Earl of Lennox. It's thought that it was Sir David de Graham (d. 1396) who built the

At the start in Milngavie

47

castle. It was certainly standing by August 1372, as evidenced by the signing there of a contemporary document. In 1505, the Grahams were created Earls of Montrose.

Sir John de Graham was of key importance in William Wallace's campaign for the independence of Scotland, while James Graham was a close ally of Rob Roy MacGregor. But it was the first Marquis, the 'Great Montrose', who became recognised as one of the finest military strategists the world has seen, following his support for King Charles I.

Allander Water, absent for a short while, resumes its pleasant presence, now stepped and providing a few gushing cascades. Boardwalks traverse a marshy area and ease the Way along through scrubland and then below a pine plantation; the pine shortly gives way to mixed woodland of larch, oak and beech.

Suddenly, on rounding a bend, Wayfarers get their first glimpse of Dumgoyne at the western end of the Campsie Fells and soon reach **Craigallian Loch**, overlooked by Craigallian House – a fine Victorian mansion.

Craigallian Loch (photo: Jonathan Williams)

Beside Craigallian Loch stands a small memorial to the Craigallian Fire, at a place where walkers from Glasgow and the surrounding area would come during the Depression years to enjoy the outdoors. The memorial marks the spot at which a campfire was kept going throughout the year.

A broad track heads on from the loch for a brief stretch of woodland once more, eventually to reach the first of a number of holiday chalets that were built around the time of World War II to provide much-needed recreational opportunity. From it, the Way bends right to pass **Carbeth Loch** – much smaller and more secluded than Craigallian Loch – where there are more chalets. The final section of this pastoral stage runs out to reach a road at a gate.

Go left along the road for about 400m and then leave it on the right for a broad grassy track, known as Tinker's Loan, flanked on either side by dilapidated dykes. The track rises slightly into a stand of beech trees, where it ends abruptly at a dyke crossed by a gate.

Suddenly, as if on a threshold, from a landscape of relative order and agreeable tranquillity walkers gaze out on a vastly different prospect – a rugged, exciting scene that rises to the long line of the Campsie Fells, with the rough escarpment of the Strathblane Hills and the knobbly upthrust of Dumgoyne especially prominent. From this point, Wayfarers move swiftly forward towards the true 'Highland' landscape that is everyone's preconceived notion of the Way, although the great Highland Boundary Fault that 'officially' marks the distinction between lowland and highland Scotland is yet to come.

The end of Tinker's Loan is indeed a threshold, for here walkers step forward from the water catchment of the great Glasgow basin and into Loch Lomond country. The far horizon embraces the rugged Crianlarich Hills – a few days away yet and accurately identifiable only by a knowledgeable eye – but attention is inevitably captured by the first glimpse of the much closer bulk of Ben Lomond, the most southerly of the Munros.

The **Campsie Fells** terminate in the west at Dumgoyne – a conical hill that is by far the shapeliest of the Campsies and stands isolated from the rest. In spite of not being the highest of the Campsie Fells, Dumgoyne, by virtue of its position, commands a fine view of distant Loch Lomond and is popular for that reason alone. Earl's Seat is the highest of the Campsie Fells, measuring 578m (1896ft). As well as being excellent walking country, the Campsie Fells have their place in history as the birthplace of Scottish skiing, when William Wilson Naismith of Glasgow – best known for conceiving Naismith's Rule for estimating the amount of time it will take to walk a route – skied the area wearing heavy Nordic-style wooden planks, becoming in 1890 (some records say 1892) the first man ever to ski in Scotland.

This end of the Campsie Fells overlooks **Strath Blane**, through which the Way now continues, but before it does it needs to work a way around the wooded volcanic plug of **Dumgoyach** (427m/1402ft). The immediate way onward leaves the gate and tackles an ongoing track that is rocky underfoot and undulates forward, dropping steadily to Arlehaven. Here, descend to go left along a rough track across moorland, targeting the left end of wooded Dumgoyach. Away to the right, a grassy ridge hosts the Dumgoyach Standing Stones – a collection of five large boulders in rough alignment that may well have first been placed here in prehistoric times, when the valley of Blane Water would have been distinctly less accommodating of the simple needs of Neolithic man.

As it begins to round Dumgoyach, the route crosses a stream that later feeds into Blane Water and rises a little before heading towards Dumgoyach Farm. Keep to the left of the farm to reach a gate and path, with open pasture on the left and a hedgerow on the right. This shepherds walkers out to meet the farm access track, which then descends easily to cross tree-flanked and fast-flowing Blane Water at Dumgoyach Bridge. A few more strides

and the route leaves the access track to turn left onto the line of a disused railway that now serves as a companion and guide for some distance (to near Gartness).

Heading for Dumgoyach – Dumgoyne in the background

The line used to be the **Blane Valley Railway**, which was opened with an optimistic, and perhaps opportunistic, eye to an early-day notion of commuter travel, especially when the line was extended northwards to Aberfoyle. The railway was opened in 1867, extended in 1882, saw the loss of passenger services in 1951, and closed completely in 1959.

The route of the Blane Valley Railway line did not escape the notice of those charged with the responsibility for locating a route for a water pipeline linking Loch Lomond and central Scotland. With intermittent presence, the pipeline, for the most part buried beneath a raised embankment, leads onward and provides an elevated and relatively dry platform during times when the main trackbed is wet.

A series of field access crossings and lanes, all guarded by metal stiles, leads ahead as the Way now plods resolutely onward down Strath Blane. ▶

At a clutch of gates there's an invitation to visit the Glengoyne Distillery, founded in 1833, but such blatant temptation would never be seriously considered by dedicated Wayfarers, would it?

Eventually, the Way runs out to meet the A81 at the site of the former **Dumgoyne** railway station, where the Beech Tree Inn – formerly a village store – offers a timely refreshment halt.

Go past the pub to a gate giving access to a busy road, turn left for a few strides, then leave the road, right, through a gate to follow the grassy margin of an elongated field. Then, by more gates and a fenced route, resume close association with the railway trackbed. More gates, more trackbed, more embankment; it all flows easily onwards to a row of cottages. Pass right and left through a stile to go behind a small industrial unit, and keep on through a brief wooded passage to emerge on a back lane.

Walkers in no hurry, or who want a short first day, could continue to Killearn, about 1.5km (1 mile) along the B834, where accommodation and refreshments may be found.

Cross the lane to a gate into sparser woodland, beyond which the proximity of Killearn Sewage Treatment Works may occasionally bring a quickening of the stride that takes you on behind the scruffy rear of a garage to continue parallel the A81.

In due course reach a farm access track, onto which the Way is briefly diverted until it dives through a gate to return to the railway trackbed, before passing under the B834. ◀

GEORGE BUCHANAN

In Killearn is a monument to George Buchanan (1506–82), a Scottish scholar and humanist, born near Killearn. Educated at a local grammar school, Buchanan was sent, at the age of 14, to study Latin, the language of the Renaissance, at the University of Paris. He came back to Scotland in 1523 and served in the army of the future King James V, later being enrolled at St Andrews as a poor student before once more visiting Paris, where he taught in the College of Sainte Barbe until 1537.

In 1537, King James appointed Buchanan tutor to one of his illegitimate sons, the future Earl of Moray, but Buchanan was charged with heresy when a satirical poem about friars offended Cardinal Beaton. Once more Buchanan found himself in France, teaching in Bordeaux (1539–42). In 1547 he was teaching in Coimbra in Portugal when he was arrested by the Inquisition as a suspected heretic.

He remained captive for four or six years (records differ), and returned to Scotland only in 1561 to be appointed classical tutor to the 19-year-old Mary, Queen of Scots, in spite of his evident inclination to Protestantism. The queen in due course gave him a sizeable pension, but he later abandoned her cause following the murder in 1567 of Lord Darnley, her husband of 18 months, when Buchanan charged her with complicity.

In 1567 he was elected moderator of the General Assembly of the Church of Scotland, then newly formed, and later became tutor to the four-year-old King James VI.

Buchanan's classic 20-volume *Rerum Scoticarum Historia* (1582) became the chief source from which foreigners gleaned their knowledge of Scotland, in spite of its unreliability. He died penniless in Edinburgh, having earned a worldwide reputation for his learning and brilliance as a scholar.

The West Highland Way presses on from the B834 through pleasant woodland at the rear of cottages before reaching the A81 once more. Cross the road with care to rejoin the Way, returning to the trackbed. But the track is now coming to an end, as far as Wayfarers are concerned, and it squeezes along between hawthorn hedgerows as it approaches a bridge up to the back road to **Gartness**. Here Wayfarers bid farewell to the old Blane Valley Railway.

Go left to Gartness, crossing Endrick Water, where sandstone cottages still emit the evocative smell of burning peat. The lane undulates in a pleasant rambling way, but nevertheless carries a regular flow of traffic, of which heavily laden Wayfarers need to be aware.

The onward route now continues in league with the road, climbing westward over the former Forth and Clyde Junction Railway, an untidy tangle of scrub that has developed since its closure in 1934. From the top of a rise near Upper Gartness Farm there's a splendid view over the farmlands of Strath Endrick and backwards to the landscapes just travelled. It's all extremely peaceful and satisfying.

The road remains your guide as it passes Easter Drumquhassle Farm (where there's a campsite and wooden wigwams). Steadily the road leads on, undulating easily, past a quarry, and finally starts to descend gently as it heads for Drymen.

Just after a sharp bend, the Way leaves the road, right, down steps to cross a stream, then follows a grassy path, climbing initially to a waymark, beyond which the continuation to reach the A811 is obvious. Leave the field by a stile at the top on the left onto the main road, where the Way goes across and to the right. Walkers staying overnight in Drymen should go left here; if you carry straight on you'll save 2km (1¼ miles).

There are two possibilities for getting to Drymen. First, instead of leaving the road following the sharp bend, keep on to meet the A811 a little closer to Drymen, cross it and climb steps to meet a minor lane leading into the village. Alternatively, having crossed the field, on reaching the A811 turn left and shortly right to follow a different way in to **Drymen**, which has a full range of facilities, a splendid hotel with excellent restaurant and leisure facilities (Buchanan Arms Hotel), and a well-stocked library/information centre, for those for whom the quest for knowledge knows no end.

DRYMEN

Drymen stands above Strath Endrick, the name deriving from *druim* – a ridge or rise – and the lands of Drymen were said to have been given to a Hungarian nobleman. Drymen, like the parish of Killearn passed through earlier in the walk, was also once part of The Lennox, an historical area associated with the Earls of Levenox or Lennox, which once included extensive tracts of Stirlingshire as well as the greater part of Dunbartonshire.

On reaching Drymen, you enter the ancient and very large parish of Buchanan. In 1621, the lands of Buchanan were annexed to the parish of Inchcailloch, and the parish enlarged so that it extended from west of Stirling to the mouth of the River Endrick, north through the middle of Loch Lomond to Island I Vow, and from there east to the head of Glen Gyle and along the upper water of Loch Katrine before heading back to the Endrick.

The earliest traces of the Lennox name are obscure, but certainly date from at least the 12th century, the name being thought to derive from *leamhanach*, meaning a 'place among elm trees'. The Lennox family were a determined breed, and, as Maurice Lindsay comments in *The Lowlands of Scotland*, few of the lords of Lennox 'died with their boots off', reigning over their domain 'with the absolute feudal sway of monarchs, and on more than one occasion, challenged the authority of the King himself'. The fifth Earl, Malcolm (1292–1333), was a solid ally of Robert the Bruce during the Wars of Independence, and came to the Bruce's aid when he sought shelter in a cave along Loch Lomond, now known as Rob Roy's Cave.

The direct line of descent ended in 1672 when the Lennox lands and title (now a dukedom) fell to Charles II, who conferred them on an illegitimate son, the sixth Duke of Lennox, who in turn passed them on to the Marquis of Montrose.

SOUTHBOUND: DRYMEN TO MILNGAVIE

Distance	12½ miles (20.2km) (from Drymen centre)
Total ascent	845ft (257m)
Total descent	835ft (255m)
Walking time	5½–6 hour
Terrain	A relatively easy conclusion to the Way, mainly on good paths, tracks and lanes with no significant ascent; railway trackbed; open pasture; woodland
Accommodation	Easter Drumquhassle, Milngavie

If there is a fault with the West Highland Way – and if there is, it's a very minor one – it's that it doesn't make a bit more use of the Campsie Fells. Instead, the route finds a way through Strath Blane, and the comparative gentleness of that line means that the last day can be fairly relaxed. The final section is a great joy – lush, fertile and gentle on the eye. The last hour, through Mugdock, is as satisfying in the north–south direction as it is motivating for those going north.

From the centre of Drymen return to the point where the West Highland Way crossed the A811, and there enter a sloping field on the right, across which steps lead up to a minor road that is followed past Easter Drumquhassle Farm and round to **Gartness**. Here join the trackbed of the Blane Valley Railway, which now guides walkers past Killearn – birthplace of George Buchanan, a

Dumgoyne from the village

Scottish scholar and humanist. Onward, the trackbed route crosses the A81 at **Dumgoyne**, where the Beech Trees Inn offers a convenient resting point, especially on a warm day.

Across the glen lies the Glengoyne Distillery, but too far off-route to tempt dedicated Wayfarers. When the trackbed clearly intercepts a farm track, turn right towards Dumgoyach Farm, rounding this and the shapely cone of Duntreath Castle. A broad path leads on to a spot marked on maps as Arlehaven (NS 535 802), and here a change of direction leads into a narrow unsurfaced lane, known as Tinker's Loan, where the route leaves Loch Lomond country and steps into the Glasgow basin. Throughout this section, the Way is dominated by the distinctive shape of Dumgoyne, a conical hill and westerly outlier of the Campsie Fells.

Follow the lane out to meet a road and turn left, walking for about 400m to a turning on the right that leads past **Carbeth Loch** and then **Craigallian Loch**, where a group of holiday chalets is encountered, built around the time of World War II. A short way further on emerge briefly on a minor road. Turn left and almost immediately right into **Mugdock Wood**. This is most agreeable, a delightful finale – lush, fecund, vibrant and ultimately in the company of Allander Water.

There is a sense that civilisation approaches, but the trees somehow manage to screen it from view until the very last moment, when walkers pop out onto a minor road. Turn right and soon walk through a small parking area and up steps to arrive, probably quite bewildered, in the very centre of **Milngavie**. Nearby stands the obelisk that marks the end of the West Highland Way.

STAGE 2
Drymen to Rowardennan

Start	Drymen road junction (NS 481 888)
Finish	Rowardennan pier (NS 359 985)
Distance	15 miles (24km); to Balmaha: 7½ miles (12km); Balmaha to Rowardennan: 7½ miles (12km)
Total ascent	2095ft (638m); to Balmaha: 1280ft (390m); Balmaha to Rowardennan: 815ft (248m)
Total descent	2215ft (675m); to Balmaha: 1400ft (427m); Balmaha to Rowardennan: 815ft (248m)
Walking time	6–7hrs
Terrain	Good tracks and paths initially through plantation then open moorland; ascent over the shoulder of Conic Hill followed by steep descent (low level alternative); then an undulating and serpentine route generally between road and loch shore; some short sections of road walking
Accommodation	Balmaha, Milarrochy, Sallochy, Rowardennan

Walkers who stayed overnight in Drymen must first to return to the point at which the Way was abandoned. In early-morning sunlight this is a refreshing start to the day, marred, only nominally, by the quirk of the route that has you heading away from your first key objective, Conic Hill. But such contrary motion is short-lived, as the route direction returns to a more expected setting once the Way is rejoined.

You may be forgiven for thinking the section of the Way from Balmaha to Rowardennan, never far from Loch Lomond, will be a gentle riparian ramble. But expect a shock, for this delightful section of the route squirms its way 'up hill and down dale' as if determined to wring every last ounce of pleasure from the experience. Preceded by easy walking in the Garadhban Forest, the route later rises quite steeply across the shoulder of Conic Hill, almost touching the summit.

Anyone breaking the day into shorter chunks and staying overnight in Balmaha will experience no particular difficulty in tackling the next stage to Rowardennan; those who have already marched in from Drymen, and for whom Balmaha is just the half-way point, may find the undulations a little wearying towards the end of the day.

On a clear day, photographers will be deliriously happy with the opportunities the walk across Conic Hill and up Loch Lomond provides to take endless pictures; natural historians will encounter a surfeit of reasons to dally; while those who delight in the simple pleasure of quality walking may just feel disposed to turn round and do it again – well, perhaps not!

In **Drymen**, directly opposite the point at which the Way emerges from the field to meet the A811, ascend a brief and narrow ramp (signposted) which rises to an old section of road. Turn right to a corner, and then pick up a path sandwiched between beech hedgerows, with open pastures and the dark stand of Garadhban Forest away to the left. The hedgerowed path is a brief interlude before

map continues on page 62

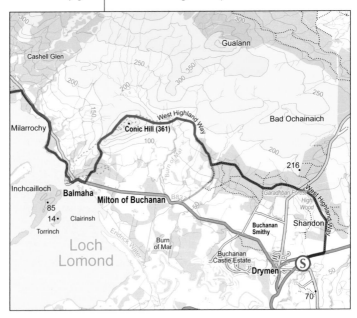

the Way pops out to run beside the A811 for a short while.

> The A811 lies along the line of a former **military road** that linked Stirling and Dumbarton – a strategically important line of communication. The road was constructed under the command of Major Caulfield between 1770 and 1784, although it is generally thought that the work amounted to little more than the realignment of an existing road; evidence, however, is scant.

At a gate on the left, leave the road. ▶ Walk ahead along the edge of an open field, and soon the Way is channelled into a gorse-lined lane that emerges into another open field before reaching the entrance to Buchanan Forest. Press on along a broad track rising to meet a main forest trail at a waymark, and bear left into the embrace of mature conifers, which are gradually being cleared.

Having risen steadily, reach a metal bar across the forest trail and immediately meet a surfaced track. Turn left and descend for a few strides before turning right into **Garadhban Forest**. Pleasant walking ensues, with fine cameos of distant hills peering above the trees and occasional glimpses of Loch Lomond. The trail starts to descend, but continues to undulate onward for a while, and, with numerous burns issuing from the forest, the sound of running water is never far distant.

In autumn, beneath the tree cover, which within strides of the trail seems dark and impenetrable, there are some fine fungal displays. Yet in spite of the denseness of the trees the forest is never oppressive – the Way travels largely at the top edge of the plantation, and there are far blue hills constantly coming and going from view.

Finally, the trail reaches its end and, at a gate as it leaves the forest, turns right. There is a now a splendid view across island-studded Loch Lomond to the hills north of Helensburgh, with the hogsback of Conic Hill away to the right, partly screened by trees.

There will be no more road walking (other than very briefly) until Balmaha on the shores of Loch Lomond – quite a comforting thought.

ROUTE NOTE

The ensuing stretch over Conic Hill involves a fair amount of ascent (although nothing excessive), so anyone seeking less strenuous passage (or saving themselves for more demanding work later in the walk) should follow the April–May diversion (below) down to Milton of Buchanan and then along the road to Balmaha.

Seasonal route variation

During a six-week (but normally four-week) period through April into May the route over Conic Hill is closed because of lambing and calving, and customarily walkers are asked to take an alternative route to avoid disturbance of stock. However, the only section that can be closed for lambing is on the eastern approach to Conic Hill, where there are two enclosed lambing fields. Under the Scottish Access Code dogs should not be taken into fields where there are lambs, calves or other young animals. So, during lambing time these fields can be closed to dogs. Information about the exact closure dates are usually published in March on www.west-highland-way. co.uk. This closure does not apply to people, only those with dogs, but it would do no harm, and probably a lot of good, to respect the farming operations by sticking closely to the path during the lambing season, or taking the well-signposted alternative route, which is not going to add time or distance to the day's walking.

Loch Lomond again features in the view – a lake that will be the source of many photographic gems over the next two days or so.

Turn towards Conic Hill, when another section of trail takes up the responsibility of leading the Way across bracken and heather moorland. The path eases on before finally reaching a deer gate and fence, with open moorland and the bracken-clad flanks of Conic Hill rising away to the left. ◄

Move on along a wide grassy path flanked by bracken. After a short sweep out onto the moors, the path swings round to begin heading for Conic Hill, preceded by the tree-lined gorge of the Burn of Mar. A good stony track strides out across the moorland, crossing Killandan

Burn – agreeably set in an attractive rowan-lined gorge – by a footbridge, before meeting a fence and stile that gives onto a path running down to the **Burn of Mar**. ▶

Immediately across the Burn of Mar bridge, a flight of steps begins the ascent across the flank of **Conic Hill**, the first significant uphill work of the route. The steps rise steeply through bracken before becoming a less demanding path through heather.

As the path rises, so Ben Lomond comes into view along with Loch Lomond, the Luss Hills and distant Ben Vorlich, Ben Vane, Ben Ime and Ben Narnain. There's no scope for missing the way on this ascent, which takes about 30 minutes to the highest point. The route does not go to the top of Conic Hill, which requires a diversion by a diagonally slanting path from the highest point of the main route; it's better to retrace the route from the summit, given the steepness of the slopes on the other side and running down to Bealach Ard.

Conic Hill lies along the Highland Boundary Fault – a great geological divide that traditionally separates Lowland Scotland from the Highlands. This

This is an ideal place, among birch and rowan, for a breather and a brew.

Highland cattle at home on the shoulder of Conic Hill before the descent to Balmaha (photo: Jonathan Williams)

fault runs for 260km (160 miles) across Scotland from Arran in the west to Stonehaven on the east coast. As you cross Bealach Ard it's possible to achieve a situation in which walkers have one foot in Lowland Scotland and another in the Highlands. It's not that simple, of course, but the fault continues through Loch Lomond, and is especially notable on one of its islands, Inchcailloch (see below). Isolated boulders on the top of Conic Hill are probably erratics, left there by the great ice sheet that completely submerged much of Britain until 10,000 years ago.

From the highest point the path descends quite steeply, and in wet conditions requires care. The views improve with every step and are a constant delight. Later, the path divides, with one arm (the one to follow) crossing the main thrust of the ridge, going left across Bealach Ard and descending even more steeply into a small

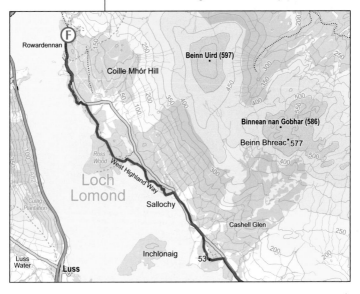

basin. It then swings round to face the fertile plains at the southern end of Loch Lomond, where the River Endrick casts about in reluctant loops before resigning itself to the inevitable and finally joining forces with the loch at a sandy spit known as Ring Point.

View of Loch Lomond from Conic Hill

The area around here forms part of the **Loch Lomond National Nature Reserve** and is a real microcosm of wildlife. It is unique for flowers and widely renowned for its wader and wildfowl populations, especially in winter when hundreds of white-fronted geese arrive from Greenland.

This richness of its wildlife and flowers did not escape the attention of Walter Scott, who in *Rob Roy* describes it as 'a fair and fertile land, [offering] one of the most surprising, beautiful and sublime spectacles in nature'.

The reserve comprises five islands and part of the adjacent mainland. The land, once cleared of forests and drained for commercial use, has been restored to more natural conditions. Walkers tackling the Way in easy stages may find time to visit

Statue of Tom Weir, countryside writer and broadcaster, at Balmaha, put up in 2014 to mark 100 years since his birth (photo: Jonathan Williams)

one of the islands, Inchcailloch, or even camp overnight on the island (providing you arrange for someone to collect you the next day!).

At the foot of the corrie, a right turn leads onto a narrow ledge above a small ravine, then the path descends a steep flight of steps that does nothing for tired or heavily laden legs and in summer is flanked by bracken and a few goat willow. As the steps end, so the path runs ahead to reach the boundary of forest – the Balmaha Plantation – at a gate.

Beyond, more steps lead down on a woodland path that soon develops into a broad trail descending amid birch and larch to a T-junction with another forest trail. Here, turn right.

The plantation is part of the much more extensive Queen Elizabeth Forest Park, and the trail through it leads out to a large car park at **Balmaha**. Go left across the car park to a toilet block and information panel, before passing on to reach the B837 and the lapping waters of **Loch Lomond** at Balmaha, opposite the welcoming Oak Tree Pub. Turn right.

The Way continues to the left of a low wall. When this ends, ignore the main road that climbs steeply on the right, but go ahead past a white cottage along a tarmac lane. Soon, at a waymark, leave the lane and climb a flight of steps into trees. Above the trees the path climbs through bracken banks to reach a horizontal path and a splendid viewpoint, known as Craigie Fort, embracing Loch Lomond and, to the right, Conic Hill, where the line of the Highland Boundary Fault is now particularly noticeable.

Move on by diving into nearby shrubbery to follow a precarious descent on wet rock and over tree roots, eventually reaching the water's edge. On arriving at an open grassy field, keep left along its bottom edge to a footbridge in a dip, rising to another field beyond. Much pleasant, if circuitous, meandering through woodland close to the shoreline leads on round Arrochymore Point and eventually leads to the shingle beach, visitor centre and car park at **Milarrochy**.

BALMAHA

Meaning 'the village by the water', Balmaha is an immensely popular place with those who find their recreation in boats, and during the summer months especially the village is well populated.

The inescapable feature of this section of the walk is the loch itself, Loch Lomond, into which river it flows. The loch was formed by the grinding action of glaciers that chiselled a deep valley and eroded the hill tops. It's 30km (18½ miles) long, 7km (4½ miles) wide at its widest point and covers 71 sq km (27½ square miles). Just north of Inversnaid it descends to a depth of 190m (623ft), while the more southerly section is only about 24m (80ft) deep.

There are 23 named islands in the loch, although some are very small, and only four of these lie further north than Luss. The loch contains some 16 species of fish, including the unusual powan – a sea fish which adapted to freshwater life when Loch Lomond was cut off from the sea as the land rose at the end of the last ice age.

Considering the prominence of this vast sheet of water, the poets have had little to say about it. Wordsworth made a token contribution, and Sir Walter Scott made a few references to the loch and its place in history; but overall its impact on the poetic mind has been singularly unimpressive, with one notable exception: the song 'Loch Lomond'. Far from being the 'love' song it might easily be supposed to be, 'Loch Lomond' is in fact a Jacobite song, and focuses on the Celtic belief that when a man dies in a foreign land his spirit returns home by the 'low road'. The passion that imbues the song is that of a man yearning for his native land.

But one perceptive observation on this topic came from the pen of Maurice Lindsay, who in *The Lowlands of Scotland* wrote, 'One reason for this dearth of written poetry is that the loch and the mountains that close in upon its northern reaches are themselves a kind of poetry: a poetry which alters subtly in form and texture with every wind that swirls around those mist-steamed Highland bens, and varies with every fresh sweep of the sun.'

So let's discover the poetry of Loch Lomond for ourselves.

INCHCAILLOCH

Walkers staying in Balmaha should seriously consider adding a day-trip to Inchcailloch to their itinerary – one of five islands managed as a national nature reserve, along with Clairinsh, Torrinch, Creinch and Aber Isle, and the mouth of the River Endrick.

There's evidence that man inhabited the loch islands as long as 7000 years ago, and certainly the tiny island called The Kitchen, to the east of Clairinsh, is the remains of a crannog – an Iron Age man-made island built about 2000 years ago.

Inchcailloch is a fascinating place, and on it is a burial ground associated with a group of nuns who lived and worshipped on the island following the death in 734 of the female Irish missionary Saint Kentigerna; she was also mother of Saint Fillan. A church dedicated to the saint was built in the early 13th century and this served the area as the parish church until 1621, when worship was transferred to the mainland.

Much of the woodland on Inchcailloch is oak, planted during the early 19th century by the Montrose estate to produce bark for tanning leather. Trees are also a dominant feature of the walk up Loch Lomond, and much of the timber produced was used for shipbuilding, houses and churches, and in the 17th century as fuel for smelting iron ore. Alder was used to clog soles and to produce charcoal for gunpowder.

Keep on between trees along the shingle, with fine views across the loch of its islands and the Luss Hills beyond. A short stretch along the road follows, before walkers leave it for a footpath on the right-hand side just a few steps away and running parallel with it. The path emerges back onto the road at Blair Bridge, but soon leaves it on the left for a western fringe section of the vast Queen Elizabeth Forest Park.

Queen Elizabeth Forest Park reaches from Loch Lomond eastwards through the Trossachs, an enormous area acquired during the 1920s, mainly from the Montrose estates. It now provides a splendid range of recreational opportunities including walking, cycling and fishing; the wildlife and flowers, too, are especially notable.

The path is never far from the road, but wanders pleasantly along, eventually crossing a stream before

Loch Lomond – on the approach to Rowardennan (photo: Jonathan Williams)

rising a little to a waymark sending walkers left and immediately right up steps into mixed woodland. A broad trail rises through the forest, formed around a small upthrust called Cnoc Buidhe. The forest becomes a mature woodland of pine, where storm-collapsed and moss-covered trees give the place an eerie feel, the gloom penetrated only by the occasional shaft of sunlight. Pine needles crunch underfoot on the descent of an elongated flight of steps, while the shadowy depths and bright interludes are food for an imaginative mind.

Before long the forest trail emerges to rejoin the road near Cashel Farm; there's a section of the Way here alongside the road, but protected from it. Just beyond the Cashel campsite, leave the road and ascend a few stone steps into woodland for a brief diversion that re-emerges onto the road near an old quarry a short distance on. Another brief woodland loop follows immediately before the route rejoins the road. Now cross the road to the loch shoreline and set off along a pathway beside a low drystone wall.

Eventually walkers are forced back onto the road near **Sallochy**, beyond which, at a waymark, ascend left into open oak woodland. This woodland is pleasant and leads down to the loch once more, but a short way on it begins a punishing little climb, including rocky steps, before crossing its highest point. Thankfully, the descent is far less demanding and much more agreeable. This happy interlude continues for some distance, never far from the shores of the loch, and in due course descends to an area to which vehicles have access. On reaching the edge of this, keep ahead on a surfaced track until you can cross a footbridge spanning an inflowing burn.

Beyond the burn the Way pushes on along the shore, passing a university boathouse and field study centre before moving steeply into **Ross Wood**. The descending path comes down to a waymark that directs walkers left along a needle-strewn pathway, finally to burst out into a felled area with a fine view of the mountains across the loch. The Way passes behind a building and reaches the shoreline again, passing a cottage and crossing a burn by a footbridge.

The ongoing footpath leads through more woodland to a second footbridge and then goes through a gap in a wall. At the top a splendid view of Ben Lomond and Ptarmigan awaits. Walkers will be relieved that here the path finally drops towards the road. ◄

Do not go to the road, but turn left into a cleared area and continue to a waymark at the far side. Go down stone steps and through tall bracken, almost touching the road again, but leave it, left, down more steps to pass round a small inlet within sight of the road. Turn left along a broad forest trail (signposted) to continue the undulating woodland way.

Finally, between rhododendron bushes, a flight of stone steps briefly rollercoasts up and down until at last, almost unbelievably, you come within sight of **Rowardennan** Pier. The path then leads out to the road. Go left along the road, which leads past the Rowardennan Hotel and the car park used by walkers bound for Ben Lomond, and peters out at the entrance to the youth hostel.

Ben Lomond (974m/3195ft) is the most southerly of the 282 Munros (as at the 2012 revision published by the Scottish Mountaineering Club), and is an excellent walk that is worth breaking your journey to undertake.

SOUTHBOUND: ROWARDENNAN TO DRYMEN

Distance	15 miles (24km)
Total ascent	2215ft (675m)
Total descent	2095ft (638m)
Walking time	6–7 hours
Terrain	Between Rowardennan and Balmaha, the Way spends a good deal of time in undulating woodland generally between a surfaced road and the loch shore. Thereafter, a steep climb leads across the shoulder of Conic Hill, before a much easier jaunt on good paths across moorland and through more plantation to Drymen
Accommodation	Sallochy, Milarrochy, Balmaha, Drymen

You may be forgiven for thinking the section of the Way from Rowardennan to Balmaha, never far from the loch, is a straightforward lochside ramble. If you do think that, you are in for a shock, for this section of the route, delightful as it is, squirms 'up hill and down dale' as if determined to wring every last ounce of pleasure from the experience. You could, of course, simply follow the road, but that would be both hazardous and monumentally boring.

Balmaha, convenient for trippers from Glasgow, is popular throughout the year, and it is a tempting halt overnight before facing the steep climb over Conic Hill.

Between Balmaha and Drymen, once Conic Hill has been dealt with, a fine section through increasingly cleared forest ensues, with the grassy embrace of Blane valley and the Campsie Fells beckoning in the distance.

At Rowardennan, just south of the hotel, take to a path branching on the right into woodland. The path is clear throughout the walk to Balmaha, but its direction is often so convoluted that it's difficult to figure out which way you're facing: should you ever find Loch Lomond on your left, then you have a problem.

The first wooded stretch is a taste of things to come, climbing across wooded hillocks, then descending to the water's edge. Ross Wood is tiring for those travelling northwards, but, with fresh legs, those who started at Rowardennan and are heading south should find it a pleasure. As the Way descends through Ross Wood, it comes down to a small bay, Camas an Losgainn.

Camas an Losgainn brings the first real chance to take in the southern section of Loch Lomond, formerly known as Loch Leven. There are 23 named islands in the loch, although some are very small, and only four of these lie further north than Luss. The loch contains some 16 species of fish, including the remarkable powan – a sea fish which adapted to freshwater life when Loch Lomond was cut off from the sea as the land rose at the end of the ice age.

To the east, Rowardennan Forest is an isolated part of the much greater Queen Elizabeth Forest Park. The Forest Park reaches from Loch Lomond eastwards through the Trossachs, an enormous area acquired during the 1920s, mainly from the Montrose estates. It now provides a splendid range of recreational opportunities, including walking, cycling and fishing; the flowers and wildlife, too, are especially notable.

As far as **Sallochy**, the Way follows the loch edge, and then runs beside the road to Cashel Farm, where it accepts the invitation to deviate into woodland once more. But the mini-bustle of Balmaha is now not far away, and although the route does its best to favour loch over roadway, taking to the lochside at every opportunity, there is an inevitability that draws walkers on around Arrochymore Point then steeply up onto the splendid viewpoint of Craigie Fort. Head across this to plunge down to the road for the final few minutes into **Balmaha** – a perfect place for a breather.

As the route leaves Balmaha and heads for Drymen it crosses a geo-logical feature known as the Highland Boundary Fault. Conic Hill, the

Loch Lomond and Ben Lomond

*first objective of the day, sits along the fault, and the contrast between
the landscape to the north and the scenery to the south is remarkable.
Suddenly everything seems more gentle and less rugged – a place where
bracken and heather eventually give way to grass and fertile pasture.*

*Other than by walking along the B837 from Balmaha via Milton of
Buchanan to Drymen – which is profoundly unthinkable – there is no
pleasurable way of avoiding Conic Hill. Those who have already walked
from Rowardennan are going to find it demanding; even fresh legs
will wobble from time to time as they ache to reach the easier ground
around the Burn of Mar on the other side.*

Cross the large car park at Balmaha, and at the rear of it locate the ongoing route climbing steeply into woodland. The woodland, but not the steepness, is short-lived as the path rises energetically through a hollow to gain the ridge line of **Conic Hill**. More climbing awaits, as the route now heads in a north-easterly direction across the flank of the hill. There's a broad, clear path all the way, and the views northwards, back the way just travelled, are a perfect excuse for regular pauses to take in the magnificent highland landscape.

*The area hereabouts forms part of the Loch Lomond National Nature
Reserve and is a real microcosm of wildlife. It is unique for flowers and
widely renowned for its wader and wildfowl populations, especially in
winter, when hundreds of white-fronted geese arrive from Greenland.*

Once the highest point of the path (but not of Conic Hill, to which a short diversion is needed to bag its summit) arrives, skitter downhill through rock and bracken to reach a bridge spanning the **Burn of Mar**. This is a great place to take a break. What's to come is straightforward and undemanding, and the Burn of Mar, in a way, represents the last lingering tang of wild places – a final place to savour the last few days.

Across the burn, a path leads through cleared plantation and then into the embrace of **Garadhban Forest**, where clearance is intermittently ongoing. Briefly walkers emerge onto a surfaced road, which is crossed to the left to regain the forest trail for what is now an easy walk out to the A811, and a last glance back to Conic Hill.

Turn right and walk alongside the A-road, shortly taking to a parallel pathway. As the path reaches a minor road, branching from the A-road, the West Highland Way turns left, crossing the A-road. But for those heading for **Drymen**, it's a simple walk along the minor road into the centre of the village.

STAGE 3
Rowardennan to Crianlarich

Start	Rowardennan pier (NS 359 985)
Finish	Crianlarich station (NN 384 250)
Distance	20 miles (32.5km); to Inversnaid: 7 miles (11.5km); to Inverarnan: 6½ miles (10.5km); to Crianlarich: 6½ miles (10.5km)
Total ascent	3330ft (1015m); to Inversnaid: 1280ft (390m); to Inverarnan: 920ft (280m); to Crianlarich: 1130ft (345m)
Total descent	2790ft (850m); to Inversnaid: 1280ft (390m); to Inverarnan: 895ft (273m); to Crianlarich: 615ft (188m)
Walking time	10–12hrs
Terrain	Mostly forestry track as far as Inversnaid, following the eastern shore of Loch Lomond with diversions onto a rocky path with crags and boulders; the section between Inversnaid and Inverarnan is by far the most demanding section of the Way, with the path following a tortuous up-and-down route along the side of Loch Lomond; onward to Crianlarich the route follows paths and tracks that are generally well-surfaced, following the course of an old military road with only moderate ascents and descents. The Way passes to the west of Crianlarich, but a branching path leads into the village.
Accommodation	Inversnaid, Ardlui, Inverarnan, Crianlarich

The stage from Rowardennan to Crianlarich is the longest day along the Way if done in its entirety, and although there have been significant footpath improvements to many stretches, it remains a demanding walk that should not be undertaken lightly, even by strong walkers – especially between Inversnaid and Inverarnan. The opportunity to break the stage, however, occurs conveniently at a couple of points (Inversnaid and Inverarnan), and there is good sense in doing this if you have the slightest doubt about your ability to tackle the complete trek comfortably.

In spite of the ruggedness, the walking throughout is of the highest quality, and there comes a tremendous feeling of satisfaction from coping with the

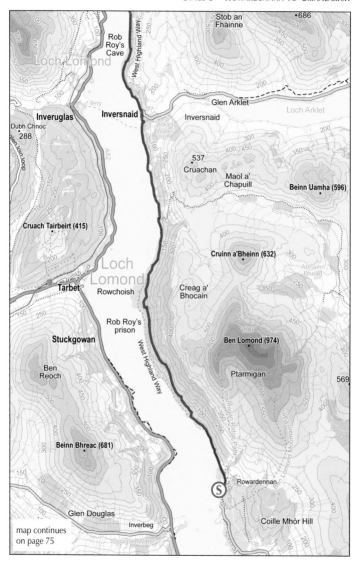

map continues
on page 75

very variable terrain, which is constantly changing as new vistas of high mountains open up. Towards the end, for those feeling weary, it is possible to finish into Crianlarich on the A82 road (and, if you want to be punctilious about following the Way in its entirety, return to the point at which you joined the road the next day). But given the 60mph speed limit on this road, it makes sense to stick to the route and keep well away from the traffic.

To continue from **Rowardennan**, start up a broad forest trail, which soon reaches Ptarmigan Lodge, named after the satellite of Ben Lomond that lies directly above. The path meanders progressively through the woodland and past Rowchoish bothy. On the way it passes a crag known as **Rob Roy's Prison**, where, according to tradition, he detained prisoners and hostages. Whether that was ever so in reality is another matter, but it serves as a timely reminder that you are now entering the lands of Clan MacGregor.

ROB ROY MACGREGOR

Romanticised by Sir Walter Scott in the novel that bears his name, and more recently given the 'Hollywood' treatment, Rob Roy MacGregor is a figure that still looms large in Scottish history; a man who led an adventurous life with, apparently, an unconventional attitude to other people's property. Born in 1671 (some accounts say 1660) in Glengyle, he was the second son of Donald MacGregor of Glengyle, a lieutenant-colonel and chief of a sept (clan) of the MacGregors. Until 1661 the Clan Gregor had for almost a century been pursued with fire and sword (during this time anyone and everyone had not only the right, but the duty, to slay, harry, burn and dispossess any MacGregors they might find without recourse to the authorities – always assuming the MacGregors let them). This was later followed by proscription of the name MacGregor so that none might legally call themselves by the name – Rob Roy himself used his mother's name, Robert MacGregor Campbell.

For more than 25 years, Rob Roy lived a relatively settled existence at Balquhidder. Nevertheless, his herds were so often plundered that he had to maintain a force of arms to defend his possessions, expanding this to

embrace his neighbours in a 17th-century protection racket. With many of his followers espousing the Jacobite cause, Rob Roy decided upon a measure of plundering of his own, and, after having purchased the lands of Inversnaid and Craigroyston, he laid claim to be chieftain of the clan. With mounting losses in cattle speculation, Rob Roy found himself at odds with the Duke of Montrose (from whom he had borrowed money) and so forfeited his lands; his houses were burned down, and his wife and children cast adrift in mid-winter. Open war between Rob Roy and the duke ensued the year after the 1715 rebellion, and a legacy of stories remains of his exploits, narrow escapes, actual escapes when captured, and of his generosity to the poor. In 1727 he was arrested and sentenced to transportation, but pardoned. He died at Inverlochlaraig on 9 January 1735.

At **Rowchoish** are the tumbled wall remains of a number of cottages that belonged to the families that lived here in the mid-18th century. More such cottages are encountered on the way to Inversnaid, but only one remains intact and inhabited.

One of the buildings has been restored by the Forestry Commission and the Scottish Rights of Way

Loch Lomond from the eastern shore

Society as a memorial to William Ferris – a founder member of the Rucksack Club, from which grew the Scottish Youth Hostels Association. Rowchoish bothy is now a useful, if basic, halt in a near perfect setting.

The broad forest trail meanwhile simply climbs steadily to its high point before easing down just as gently. ▶

Eventually, the broad trail comes to an end and collapses into a woodland pathway of considerable pleasure. Oak, birch and pine provoke shifting shadows and dappled delights as walkers move along, not to mention a continuing downpour long after rain has stopped. At a small burn, the Way reaches the base of a bracken-clad slope with fewer trees, but beyond this brief interlude it returns to the greenery before finally quitting the Queen Elizabeth Forest Park at the **Cailness Burn**. Close by stands Cailness Cottage.

Cross Cailness Burn by a large footbridge that stands on the site of at least two previously demolished bridges that were swept aside in 1975 and 1985. The Way eases on towards Inversnaid, waymarked whenever it's needed, and passes through pleasant woodland well populated

The opportunity occurs a few times to savour a stunning canvas in which triple-peaked Ben Arthur, better known as The Cobbler, and the nearby Ben Narnain are portrayed to superb effect.

Loch Lomond at Inversnaid

with birdlife. After a few small rises, all lost again, the Way finally rounds a small rock buttress falling into the loch and arrives quite suddenly at the first of two bridges that lead across Snaid Burn and its attractive waterfall to the car park of the Inversnaid Hotel at **Inversnaid**.

ROUTE NOTE

The stretch of the Way between Inversnaid and Inverarnan has long held a reputation for being the most difficult part of the whole walk. In the mid-1990s, however, some improvements were made to the pathway, now hardly noticeable, and these have significantly eased the difficulties. Even so, it is not the easiest of sections and will require concentration throughout, especially since it still involves a fair amount of strenuous undulating walking and has a few rocky sections to contend with. Once the route moves away from the loch shore, however, these difficulties end and much easier walking ensues.

Go in front of the Inversnaid Hotel and cross the car park to a WHW signpost, there entering the Royal Society for the Protection of Birds nature trail – a further reminder of the wealth of birdlife you can expect to find along this wooded eastern shore of Loch Lomond.

Start along a gravel path (in front of a toilet block) that soon enters oak woodland. A short way on, the route passes a boathouse, from where there is a splendid view across the loch of Ben Vorlich, Ben Vane and, further south, Ben Narnain. The Way then rises on a narrow path through bracken to a small burn and footbridge, where the RSPB trail climbs to the right and the Way crosses the bridge to the left.

The continuing path tackles a short cliff, at the base of which a large tumble of boulders has created the cavern known as Rob Roy's Cave, which will require a brief diversion and some finding amid the confused terrain.

In spite of the **cave**'s association with Rob Roy, who may indeed have used it, there is a claim, too, that it was once named after Robert the Bruce, who is said to have sheltered there following defeats in battle at Methven and Dalrigh.

Beyond the cave the rugged going persists as the Way plunges onward, casting about from gravelly shoreline to woodland stretches. Here, help lies only back the way you came or ahead at Inverarnan, and in poor weather conditions it can feel very isolated. Nor does the feeling go away for some time as the route penetrates further up the glen, passing a long-abandoned croft at Pollochro and on to reach the Allt Rostan opposite Island I Vow. Here, at a fence, walkers leave one county (Stirling) and enter another (Argyll and Bute).

More scrambling progress is needed before, with a delightful sense of relief, the difficulties end on the approach to the open bay a short distance south of Doune. Beyond the burn that flows into the loch at this point, the Way begins an easy and pleasant ascent, keeping largely to open ground as it treks across to **Doune**, where there are two buildings – one a bothy, the other a farmhouse. It is a splendid location, and travellers along the A82 on the far side of the loch must be envious as they look across to the stark white building and walkers lounging around in a state of evident contentment.

Heading for upper Loch Lomond

Lochside wandering follows as the route presses on towards Ardleish. ◄ Continuing above Ardleish Farm, the Way climbs across a small ridge and runs on to cross a dyke by a stile before easing up to a shallow glen to the east of **Cnap Mor** and down to Dubh Lochan.

Just south of Ardleish, anyone wanting to escape could go down to the shore and hoist a cone to summon a ferry from the other side.

Cnap Mor is something of a threshold on this section of the walk. It's here that with little or no ceremony walkers move from what is essentially the Loch Lomond basin into Glen Falloch, its northerly sibling. After so much delightful walking in its company, as you bid farewell to the great loch you're entitled to express a few appropriate words on the experience!

For a short while the Way seems reluctant to descend from Dubh Lochan, maintaining a lofty air with the trinity of Munros – Beinn Lui, Beinn Oss and Beinn Dubhcraig – towering over the moors of Glen Falloch in splendid fashion. Finally, the path does begin to descend, easing companionably through woodland to emerge onto level ground just south of **Ben Glas Burn**. A bridge leading immediately to a stile finally brings walkers to Beinglas Farm. ◄

Above the bridge the Ben Glas Burn often performs a series of spectacular falls and slides, although they are not best seen from the Way.

This was once a passage well used by drovers, and the Inverarnan Hotel is a former cattle drovers' inn. Traditionally, drovers would meet at the northern end of Loch Lomond, and while the Crieff tryst (cattle market) flourished **Glen Falloch** was the quickest way of joining the route from Skye, at the top of Glendochart. Once the Falkirk tryst assumed prominence, around 1770, the route up Glen Falloch saw much less traffic. Another route crossed the River Falloch near this point and traversed the hills to the east of Ardlui to reach Glen Gyle. In *A Tour in the Highlands* (1803) James Hogg, the Ettrick Shepherd, described using this route for droving sheep.

Glen Falloch is a splendid continuation of the Way – a complete contrast to what has gone before. The river, which is the Way's companion for a while, is a succession of cascades, white-water hollows and rapids, and after heavy rain is an especially fearsome sight. The terrain is a constantly changing scene of open moorland pastures and wooded stands of birch, oak and rowan, and is never dull for a moment.

On reaching Beinglas Farm (an overnight stop much improved in recent years and now providing a good range of accommodation, refreshment and a gear shop), bear right to a gate at the foot of a path that steeply climbs the hillside above and is a popular route to Beinn Chabhair. Ignore this tempting diversion and go left along a broad stony access track until, on approaching the main road, it is possible to leave the track, branching right on a rocky path.

With a little rough going in the wooded areas, the Way generally continues uneventfully on its journey, passing ruined cottages at Blackcroft that wishful thinking might have you believing is Derrydarroch. For a while, the onward line is a little doubtful if you don't spot the tall waymark at a bridge. But beyond that, a much more substantial track leads on and eventually down to **Derrydarroch**, sheltered in a little hollow. ▸

Significant construction work on a new hydro-electric plant was affecting the route here in 2015. Immediately after Derrydarroch cross the Falloch at Derrydarroch Bridge and turn right to traverse a small birch-clad hillock before descending to a constructed path running parallel with the river. About ½ mile (1km) from Derrydarroch the path swings left and passes under the railway line by a low cattle creep, an inelegant and strenuous experience for walkers with large packs. With far greater simplicity than any written description can render, the Way, ignoring steps just beyond the railway, joins the old road for a while and then works round to pass beneath the modern A82 by a tunnel to steps that lead up to the old military road which is the onward guide to Crianlarich.

As Wayfarers progress up the glen, so the incidence of isolated pine trees grows. These are remnants of the great ancient Caledonian pine forest that covered this entire area following the last ice age.

Many parts of the highlands are criss-crossed with **military roads** – the vast majority inaccurately ascribed to General Wade. In reality it was his some-time Inspector of Roads, Major William Caulfield, who supervised the construction of many of the roads, notably from 1740, when General Wade left Scotland, until his death in 1767. It was Caulfield who was responsible for all the military roads used by the West Highland Way, and his contribution amounted to something over 800 miles (1300km).

In spite of all his efforts, Major Caulfield was destined to live in the shadow of the general, and even today you hear people speaking of Wade roads when referring to roads built by Caulfield. Caulfield, in truth, built three times as many roads as General Wade, but always gave the general full credit as the originator of the concept. Even so, it is probably fair to say that Caulfield made a greater impact on the communication network in Scotland than anyone.

Beyond the A82, the line of the old military road rises steadily above the glen as it passes Keilator Farm. It then reaches a gate and meeting of pathways at the edge of the woodland to the west of Crianlarich, where there are a number of choices.

The West Highland Way here turns left. The most direct way of reaching the main road is ahead, down the initially squelchy Bogle Glen. As walkers reach and cross the stile at the head of Bogle Glen, so they step for the first of four times across the British watershed – to the south the waters drain into the Loch Lomond catchment; to the north they are part of the Tay system and flow ultimately into the North Sea.

The **British watershed** has nothing to do with television; it is an almost imaginary line running the length of Britain. If a drop of rain were to fall on the watershed precisely, it would be divided equally – half would flow to the North Sea and the other half to the Irish Sea. The precise line of the watershed is, of course, difficult to determine, but there are places where it's obvious that it must exist. The approximate length of the watershed, should anyone feel tempted to walk it, is in the region of 1800 miles (2900km).

It is more usual, however, for Wayfarers to take a break at **Crianlarich**, and by turning right at the gate to follow a steadily descending path through woodland and the walkers' tunnel beneath the Crianlarich bypass, with fine views of Ben More, Stobinian and Cruach Ardrain, which emerges onto the old road. From here it's left 200m to the station. Walkers bound for the youth hostel or village centre should take the path that goes under the railway line.

CRIANLARICH

Crianlarich lies at the place where traditional through-routes west–east and north–south meet, and rests forever beneath the gaze of Ben More, along the southern flank of Strath Fillan. It's a village of perpetual activity that largely owes its present-day prominence to its railway connections. It's an unavoidable location for motorised and railway travellers bound for the Western Highlands and beyond, and is splendidly placed for walkers who are intent on gathering the great summits of the Southern Highlands. The village offers a wide range of B&B facilities, while the youth hostel must rank among the best in the catalogue of the SYHA.

It is not clear how the name of the village originated. Some authorities suggest it derives from Craobh an Lairig, meaning the 'tree by the pass', and while on the face of it this seems logical, much would depend on how long the name has been in use, since much of this area was part of the Caledonian pine forest. It would seem unusual, then, to single out one tree for special attention.

Crianlarich also has the added attraction for Wayfarers of being roughly halfway along, with (by common consensus) the more difficult part already completed. But accept that comment advisedly, as the West Highland Way has its own repertoire of dirty tricks, some of which are played out on Rannoch Moor and across the rugged countryside that leads down to, and on from, Kinlochleven. Do not be lulled into thinking everything is now a few days' easy walking.

SOUTHBOUND: CRIANLARICH TO ROWARDENNAN

Distance	20 miles (32.5km)
Total ascent	2790ft (850m)
Total descent	3330ft (850m)
Walking time	10–12 hours
Terrain	Rough tracks and moderate ascents and descents along an old military road to begin with, starting with a steep climb out of Crianlarich. The section between Inverarnan and Inversnaid is by far the most demanding stretch of the entire route with the path following an up-and-down route alongside Loch Lomond. Thereafter, forest tracks lead from Inversnaid to Rowardennan.
Accommodation	Inverarnan, Ardlui, Inversnaid, Rowardennan

Taken in its entirety, the stage from Crianlarich to Rowardennan is the longest day along the Way, and although there have been significant footpath improvements to many stretches, it remains a demanding walk that should not be undertaken lightly, even by strong walkers. The opportunity to break the stage, however, occurs conveniently at a couple of points (at Inverarnan and Inversnaid), and there is good sense in doing so if time is not of the essence.

In spite of the ruggedness, the walking throughout is of the highest quality passing as it does through magnificent landscapes and hemmed in by

Looking into Glen Falloch from the head of Bogle Glen

high mountains, and there comes a tremendous feeling of satisfaction from coping with the very variable terrain.

Head up the old section of the A82 for about 250m until a new path on the right leads to the walkers' tunnel under the new section of road (completed in 2014), and up through woodland to the head of Bogle Glen. There, having rejoined the main line of the route, turn left through a gate onto a rough track that leads above Keilator Farm, still, it should be noted, following the course of Caulfield's military road. The first section follows **Glen Falloch**, and there are fine views to the south of An Caisteal and Beinn Chabhair.

The ongoing track eventually leads to a very low tunnel, by means of which walkers pass beneath the A82 and the railway line beyond, to continue uneventfully to **Derrydaroch**. From here the route is never far from the glen river, crossing it at Derrydaroch Bridge and soon passing the Falls of Falloch, and staying more or less parallel with the river all the way to Beinglas Farm at Inverarnan. Directly above the farm, the Ben Glas Burn produces impressive waterfalls.

South from Beinglas the route is never in doubt, but gives some of the most difficult walking – especially for those with heavy packs. Within a short distance, the river bears away from the path, which now climbs to pass through a gap between a low hill, Cnap Mor, and the high Munros to the east.

Cnap Mor is a significant point, that at which Wayfarers leave the rugged delights of Glen Falloch for those of the Loch Lomond basin. The great loch lies immediately ahead, and arrival here, at Ardleish Farm, should be treated with some minor form of celebration. In a sense, you are on the final leg, albeit with some way still to go.

The route now follows the shoreline of Loch Lomond all the way to the unexpected hotel at **Inversnaid**. The going is not the easiest, although it is easier following improvements than it has been for some years.

The onward section, south from Inversnaid, continues to call for care and attention until, not far from the bothy at Rowchoish, Wayfarers reach the end of a broad forest trail, which now leads easily out to **Rowardennan**.

On the way the route passes a crag known as Rob Roy's Prison, where, according to legend, he held prisoners and hostages. Whether that was ever so in reality is another matter, but it serves as a timely reminder that the Way has been passing through the lands of Clan MacGregor.

STAGE 4
Crianlarich to Bridge of Orchy

Start	Crianlarich station (NN 384 250)
Finish	Junction with A82, Bridge of Orchy (NN 297 396)
Distance	13¼ miles (21.3km); to Tyndrum: 6¾ miles (10.8km); to Bridge of Orchy: 6½ miles (10.5km)
Total ascent	1515ft (462m); to Tyndrum: 1070ft (327m); to Bridge of Orchy: 445ft (135m)
Total descent	1590ft (484m); to Tyndrum: 900ft (275m); to Bridge of Orchy: 690ft (210m)
Walking time	7hrs
Terrain	A stiff climb out of Crianlarich leads onto clear paths and tracks through woodland before heading down to the valley and an easy looping walk into Tyndrum, twice crossing the main road. A gentle ascent then wanders up alongside the railway to cross the British watershed before a long and easy descent through the wide open valleys of Auch Glen.
Accommodation	Strathfillan, Tyndrum, Bridge of Orchy

En route to Tyndrum the West Highland Way casts about on both sides of Strath Fillan, as if trying to take in all the best bits, but in reality taking the easiest line. Any preconceived notion that the section begins with densely packed woodland will be instantly dispelled as the Way threads a course that provides a host of enticing vistas through the trees and a fine balcony walk high above the glen.

As it crosses the road and visits the site of St Fillan's Priory, so the Way steps back in time, before returning to the riverside comfort of the Fillan's banks and a pleasant stretch close by the Crom Allt into Tyndrum. Between here and Bridge of Orchy the route enjoys wide views of fine mountains and sweeping glens.

From **Crianlarich**, return to the old military road – either by a steady climb from the car park near the railway

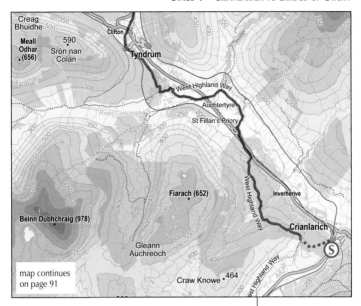

station or via Bogle Glen starting a short distance along the road to Tyndrum. ▶

From the head of Bogle Glen start ascending on a good path skirting the edge of a larch plantation to the top of a small rise, beyond which the path dips to the left before ascending again, now flanked by trees. The path undulates onwards, in and out of trees and gradually gaining height, with the view northwards over Strath Fillan to Ben Challum improving with every stride.

For a while the path effects a pleasant promenade high above the glen, and gradually works a way down to cross Herive Burn by a wooden footbridge. Thereafter, the path rises to join a broader forest trail at a waymark, with the route here branching right. ▶ At the branching path for Ewich Farm (at a waymark), keep left onto a narrow path through a pleasant spread of broom, beside a stream. The path is ultimately deflected right by the Allt an t-Saoir and runs down through larch to pass beneath

Both points are signposted, and both provide superb views of the ring of mountains to the south and south-east of Crianlarich.

The retrospective view now embraces Stobinian, which until now had sheltered coyly behind intervening heights.

the railway bridge on the Oban branch line. Beyond the bridge, the Way reaches what remains of the old glen road, and turns left along it to cross the burn and pick up a gravel track leading out to the present-day road.

Cross the busy road with care and go instantly left along a narrow path above a wooded embankment. The path leads to a stile, beyond which the route diagonally crosses a pasture to the bridge spanning the **River Fillan**. Now the Way runs up towards Kirkton Farm, turning left just before reaching it to swing round to the site of St Fillan's Priory.

St Fillan's Priory remains

The priory here was probably a 12th-century monastic site dedicated to the memory of **St Fillan**, an Irish monk, son of St Kentigerna. Many tales have been handed down of his exemplary life during the 8th century.

Not too far away is the battle site of Dalrigh, where Robert the Bruce suffered a defeat in 1306. It was following this that Bruce granted the monastic settlement the status of priory – logically, it might be assumed, because he received spiritual support

from the monks following his defeat. The true site of the priory is thought to be closer to the Holy Pool, a short distance upriver.

The most widespread of the tales about St Fillan concerns a sign given to Robert the Bruce as he prepared for the Battle of Bannockburn. The accounts tell how a relic of the saint, an arm bone in silver, had been brought to the battlefield as a token of good fortune. As Bruce kneeled, praying before it, the case opened to reveal the relic, much to the astonishment of its guardian, who sensibly had brought only an empty case to Bannockburn.

From the priory, cross a cattle grid and go along a broad track that leads to **Auchtertyre** Farm. Beyond this, cross the Allt Auchtertyre and turn left to walk out to rejoin the A82, near the Holy Pool.

The **Holy Pool** (just a short distance off the Way) is said to be the original site of St Fillan's Priory, and the place where insane persons were bathed in the chilly waters before being taken to the chapel to be tied up all night to the font – a treatment that also involved St Fillan's bell being placed over the head of the person. No records seem to exist to suggest that the treatment actually cured anyone.

Cross the road (although a nearby underpass is preferable) and press on down a rough track accompanied by the river. The path swings round to reach a surfaced lane near a bridge. Walk straight across the lane (waymark) and keep going on a track parallel with the river. On crossing an inflowing stream, immediately branch right on a path that for a short while pursues a very pleasant course beside the river. The route then branches right again on a broad track, which very soon it leaves for a path on the left that cuts across a boggy corner to meet another broad track going left. The Way comes down to cross the Crom Allt by a wooden bridge, near the site known as Dal Righ, 'the King's Field'.

At Dalrigh, Glen Fillan

It was at **Dalrigh** that Robert the Bruce is said to have engaged the MacDougalls of Lorne in battle, and to have been defeated. This occurred during an unhappy period, in 1306, following closely on his crowning as King of Scotland, when he was also defeated by English forces at Methven, near Perth, as a result of which he took to the hills with a small group of supporters.

Press on with the track for a short distance then leave it on the right, at a waymark, for a narrow stony footpath that rises to pass a small lochan.

This delightful pool of water is known as the **Lochan of the Lost Sword** – a reference to the legend that, following his defeat at Dalrigh, Bruce cast his sword into the water. There are other versions of the same tale, some suggesting that it was William Wallace and not Robert the Bruce. Neither of these legends has much historic credibility.

From the pool, the path rambles on uneventfully to reach a derelict area of land marking the site of a foundry where lead ore, brought down from the mountains,

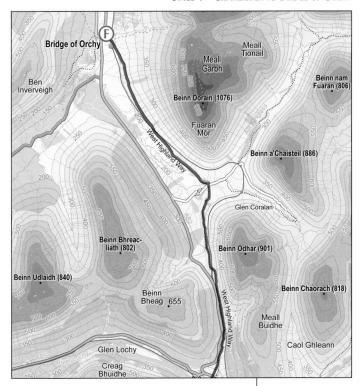

was crushed prior to being transported to Alloa. Once across this barren expanse, at a gate, enter woodland once more, now at the edge of the developed area that has grown around **Tyndrum**. A waymark directs up into woodland for the last serious encounter with trees until the final stages of the walk, and on beside the river.

Continue to a group of cottages and a surfaced lane. Turn left on reaching the lane (although by turning right the facilities of Tyndrum are reached a little quicker than by following the Way), and follow this round towards Lower Tyndrum station. Leave the path on the right before reaching the station, and take a path doubling towards the river and heading towards Tyndrum. A brief encounter with a shallow burn may leave you a little wetter before you stroll up in front of cottages to reach the main road.

TYNDRUM

Once mistakenly thought to have been one of the highest inhabited villages in northern Britain, Tyndrum has grown enormously (some would say out of all proportion) in the past 30 or more years.

Tyndrum, 'the house on the ridge', was an 18th- and 19th-century 'service station' much favoured by cattle drovers. The village was one of a number of overnight rest halts, or 'stances', usually at intervals of 10 miles, encountered along what is now the West Highland Way – others were Inveroran and Altnafeadh, at the entrance to Glen Coe. Little seems to have changed, for Tyndrum is still very much a resting place on the highland tourist route, and only those with eyes for the hills seem to look upon the village as anything more than a single night's halt.

From Tyndrum to Bridge of Orchy the main land uses are the growing of trees in plantations and the raising of sheep and cattle. Beyond Forest Lodge at the western end of Loch Tulla, grass and heather dominate the landscape. This is red deer country, and while the deer graze high during the summer months, in early spring and late autumn you stand a good chance of seeing them at lower levels.

Picking up the trail at the main road, go ahead up a surfaced lane beside a burn. When the lane ends, a broad stony track rises up the glen to a gate and stile, running close to the A82 for a while. It presses on, never far from the road, and climbs very steadily to the regional boundary at another gate and stile, once more crossing the British watershed. From the stile keep to the path, which ascends a little further, slightly to the right beneath the southern slopes of **Beinn Odhar**, with the shapely cone of Beinn Dorain directly ahead, set against the further heights of Black Mount.

The track continues to ascend for a short while, and then levels before beginning the long descent into Auch Gleann (more correctly Gleann Achadh-innis Chailein). Before long the track drops steeply to the left

Shapely Beinn Dorain on the run down to Bridge of Orchy

to cross beneath the railway line, beyond which it joins a broader track leading down from the main road near the watershed.

Striding into the glen provides a tremendous, invigorating sense of openness and freedom, with the great sweeping sides of Beinn Dorain to draw the eye. Gradually the path descends to a farm, close by which walkers cross the glen river, the **Allt Kinglass**, by a single-arch bridge. Over the bridge, turn left on a farm track. A short way on, a small wooded riverside glade invites a break before you resume the trek below the high crags and gullies of Beinn Dorain on the way to **Bridge of Orchy station**. ▶ When the track reaches the station, branch left at a waymark sign through a metal gate and go under the railway line to the A82 road.

Having travelled in the company of the railway since Glen Falloch, the Way now abandons the line, which it doesn't meet again until journey's end at Fort William. With a similar desire to shun the transport trappings of modern society, the Way shortly quits the main road, which it will not rejoin until it reaches the entrance to Glen Coe. Turn right and go down the lane to reach the A82 road and the **Bridge of Orchy** Hotel.

There can be no error of route-finding here – the glen is high, wide and handsome, and the way forward clear enough to follow on the darkest of nights.

SOUTHBOUND: BRIDGE OF ORCHY TO CRIANLARICH

Distance	13¼ miles (21.3km)
Total ascent	1590ft (484m)
Total descent	7 hours
Terrain	A long and steady pull on a broad track through Auch Glen to the county boundary and watershed feeds into an easy descent to Tyndrum. Low level walking ensues for a while before the Way climbs into forest on a clear path but with numerous undulations and twists and turns before the branching path down to Crianlarich
Accommodation	Tyndrum, Strathfillan, Crianlarich

The stretch that leads to Tyndrum is truly splendid, beginning with a long and gradual climb as far as the river issuing from Gleann Achadh-innis Chailein. More climbing ensues across the sweeping western slopes of Beinn Odhar to arrive once more on the British watershed (see South to North, Section 3) close by the A82.

Because stopping at Tyndrum makes only a short day, many walkers continue to Crianlarich, giving a longer and more satisfying day, but with most of the hard work in the latter stages as the route climbs into forest above Strath Fillan.

Approaching Tyndrum

Cross the A-road at Bridge of Orchy and follow the lane up to the station underpass, beyond which walkers pass through a gate giving onto the military road. A steady but gentle ascent heralds a long and delightful walk to the bridge spanning the **Allt Kinglass**. This is relaxed walking, and a good time to take it easy and conserve energy.

From the Allt Kinglass, the Way starts to rise more enthusiastically as it angles above the Allt Coire Chailein. Gradually, the track closes in on the glen A-road to the right. As it does so, keep an eye open for a branching path, over a stile on the left, that climbs steeply to pass beneath the railway line, and then onward and gently upward to the bealach marking the watershed. Now it is all downhill to Tyndrum, a splendid and easy romp that concludes at the edge of town, once believed to be the highest inhabited village in the highlands.

Between Tyndrum and Crianlarich, the Way follows the course of Strath Fillan, briefly in the company of the river, but more usually on one side or the other. In terms of distance, this stretch is just the same as that from Bridge of Orchy to Tyndrum, and the two can be usefully combined to give a splendid and enjoyable day. Initially the Way enjoys easy walking as it leaves Tyndrum, but later, beyond Auchtertyre Farm, having recrossed the A82, the route takes to the wooded slopes that flank the eastern side of Fiarach and brings a period of undulations that can be tiring.

Resume the walk from the crossing point of the A82 in Tyndrum and walk down past a row of cottages. Then cross low-lying rough pasture and follow a clear path up to join a road end close by Tyndrum's south station, on the Oban line.

Follow the lane for a short distance until it's possible to branch right, just as the lane swings to the left. The path now heads for the river, which it accompanies for a while, and then crosses a bleak expanse where once

lead mining took place. Cross this and resume easy walking through bracken and heather with a scattering of birch. The path is clear throughout and leads past the Lochan of the Lost Sword eventually to a broad track, west of Dalrigh.

Memorial to the Legend of the Lost Sword

There is potential for confusion now, as the path meanders on, but, as elsewhere, the West Highland Way is sensitively waymarked, with discreet waymarks appearing whenever you need them. Beyond Dalrigh, the landscape opens up, and the route almost immediately joins the riverbank and follows it out to re-cross the A82 (preferably by using a convenient underpass on the right).

Beyond the A-road, a broad track leads to Auchtertyre Farm, there bearing right to head for Kirkton Farm and passing the site of **St Fillan's Priory** on the way.

Passing Kirkton Farm, turn right and walk to a bridge spanning the **River Fillan**. On the far side of the bridge, cross a stile and cut across a field to walk parallel with the A-road for a short distance before crossing it again, although this time there is no protective underpass. Once across, there's a brief skirmish with light birch woodland as the route follows the old glen road to a bridge directly below the much higher railway bridge.

This is where the more difficult part of the day begins as the route climbs beneath the railway bridge high into woodland, always following a clear path, but there are numerous undulations and changes of direction to deal with. Thankfully, there is no scope for error as the path is straightforward and waymarked when necessary. There may be a moment of doubt at a branching path for Ewich Farm, but the onward route is the clearer of two options and presses on through forest to cross Herive Burn. After this it climbs steeply to gain what turns out to be a fine terraced path high above the glen, with virtually all ascent now ended.

Gradually, the path descends; ahead, beyond Crianlarich, lie the huge mounds of Ben More and Stobinian. A final downward flourish leads to the head of the shallow Bogle Glen – a direct but boggy way down to the A-road. On reaching the head of the glen, the West Highland Way turns southwards, through a gate, and it's to this point that walkers staying overnight in Crianlarich will have to return.

To reach Crianlarich, cross the top of Bogle Glen, ignoring the gate, and follow a clear, ongoing path that threads a way through woodland to pass beneath the Crianlarich bypass by a walkers' tunnel, and then descend to the old A82, not far from **Crianlarich railway station**. Walkers bound for the youth hostel or village centre should take the path that goes under the railway line.

STAGE 5

Bridge of Orchy to Kingshouse

Start	Junction with A82, Bridge of Orchy (NN 297 396)
Finish	King's House Hotel (NN 259 546)
Distance	12 miles (19.4km)
Total ascent	1615ft (493m)
Total descent	1335ft (407m)
Walking time	5–6hrs
Terrain	A short uphill section (avoidable by following the road) then descends to the start of Rannoch Moor at Forest Lodge, across which a generally broad, stony track leads on at an easy gradient. This can be a very exposed section in poor weather, with high mountains on the one hand and open moorland on the other, and there is no shelter until the White Corries Ski Centre.
Accommodation	Inveroran, Kingshouse

Between Bridge of Orchy and the King's House Hotel at the eastern end of Glen Coe, the Way provides the opportunity to stride out purposefully across Rannoch Moor, with either the old Glen Coe road or one of Caulfield's military roads underfoot. On one hand, the moor itself slips away into the endless blue oblivion of the eastern horizon; on the other, a stunning wall of mountains is a constant shepherd, guiding you easily along the broad trail, yet at the same time is a blatant and beguiling temptation to escape into the tantalising summits of Black Mount.

The walking in this section is easy throughout, but should not be underestimated. On Rannoch Moor walkers reach a point as far away from civilisation as anywhere else on the Way, and in poor weather conditions it can be one of the most inhospitable places in Scotland. Long stony sections of the trail can be uncomfortable underfoot.

At **Bridge of Orchy** stay on the lane that runs down beside the hotel to cross the River Orchy by a substantial bridge, built about 1750. Anyone who chances by here

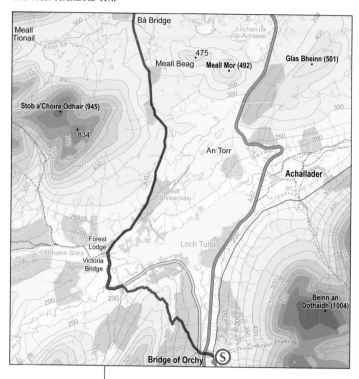

map continues on page
101

when the Orchy is at its most turbulent cannot fail to marvel at the ingenuity of the bridge engineers in overcoming the problems the river would have posed.

ROUTE NOTE

Between Bridge of Orchy and the start of the crossing of Rannoch Moor lies a brief woodland and hilltop interlude followed by a stunning descent to Inveroran and Forest Lodge at the western end of Loch Tulla. Tired walkers, or those simply wanting to take it easy, can just follow the road, but the climb to Màm Carraigh at the northern end of Ben Inverveigh is nothing like as difficult as might be supposed, and any weariness is offset in great measure by a panorama of towering summits that improves with every upward step, reaching a climax at the top of the pass. The view of Stob Gabhar, Stob Choire Odhair and their attendants alone more than justifies this modest little climb.

Just after the bridge, leave the road at a waymark and ascend on a path rising easily into woodland. When the path breaks free at the top of the forest it swings to the left, still rising at a comfortable gradient, with the view to the east dominated by Beinn Dorain and Beinn an Dothaidh. Onward, the path (the old military road) rises amid grassy hillsides studded with heather. As it climbs, so the path swings around and begins a pleasant traverse of the northern hillside of **Ben Inverveigh**, with excellent views, away to the right, of Loch Tulla.

Finally, as it crosses a shoulder, a large cairn at the end of the ridge on the right provides a splendid viewpoint of the loch, Forest Lodge and the sprawling mass of granite mountains beyond. ▸ The track thereafter descends without difficulty to rejoin the road near the Inveroran Hotel.

Photographers will find that another cairn and a single rowan tree, just below the top of the ridge, offer an attractive foreground to go with that amazing background.

William and Dorothy Wordsworth, in company with a south-bound cattle drove, stayed at the **Inveroran Hotel** in September 1803, although they were less than complimentary about the food they received there. Even so, Dorothy was moved to write evocatively of the inn filled with 'seven or eight travellers, probably drovers, with as many dogs, sitting in a complete circle round a large peat fire in the middle of the floor, each with a mess of porridge in a wooden vessel on his knee'.

DROVING

The raising and selling of cattle was a key element in the fragile economies of 18th- and 19th-century Scotland, but the story of Scotland's cattle goes much further back. Long before man learned to till the earth, the grazing of livestock was his principal means of livelihood, and early records bear testimony to the vast numbers of sheep and cattle in Scotland and the importance of grazing.

Breeding and raising cattle was difficult enough, but selling them presented its own problems, since there were few markets and most of these lay many miles away – in Falkirk and Doune, for example. As the cattle business developed, the only way to get cattle to market was to walk them there under the experienced eye of teams of drovers. From places as distant as the Outer Hebrides, Skye, Mull and Ardnamurchan, the cattle would be brought to the southern markets, via Spean Bridge and Fort William, before heading for Kingshouse, Rannoch Moor, Inveroran and Tyndrum. A good part of the West Highland Way pursues these ancient droving routes, so it's fitting that they should be perpetuated in this way.

One curious feature of the droving was the 'shoeing' of cattle – a necessity carried out in just the same way that today we shoe horses. The idea of shoeing cattle just to get them to market may seem strange, but lame cattle were unlikely to command the best prices, assuming they reached the market at all.

Go left now and follow the road to the bridge spanning the Allt Tolaghan, the ground beside which provides

The Black Mount summits viewed across Loch na h-Achlaise from the A82

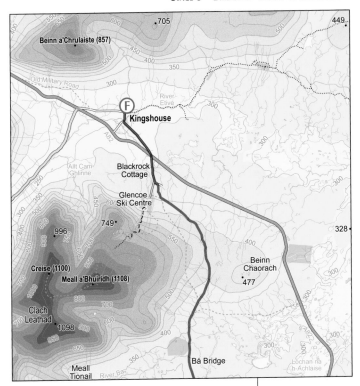

a splendid wild campsite. Onward, the road runs forward to **Forest Lodge**, a former hunting lodge. It's here that the Way, for a while, abandons the military road, electing instead to pursue the course of the old Glen Coe road, which begins through the gate at Forest Lodge.

What lies beyond Forest Lodge is the magic that is **Black Mount** and Rannoch Moor – a fantastic upland plateau of heathered braes, sweeping moorlands, rivers, burns and lochs of all shapes and sizes. In the right conditions, it is quite simply a wonderland, but one that could become a nightmare with any adverse change to the conditions. ▶

The distance from Forest Lodge to Blackrock Cottage is 8 miles (13km), making the point of no return Bà Bridge; beyond that you keep going.

There is some suggestion that the onward **route across Rannoch** may not be the line of the old Rannoch drove road, an opinion expressed in *Roads, Tracks and their Interpretation* by Brian Paul Hindle, which opts for the drovers using 'the other shore of Loch Tulla'. Such a course, however, would not feed the drove into Inveroran, which was known to be a principal overnight halt.

But what is known is that much of the road across Rannoch was improved and maintained by Thomas Telford after 1803, when he was appointed by the government of the day to oversee the building of roads in the highlands. For a time, he may have found himself with the unenviable responsibility of bringing about a planned road across Rannoch from Killin to Spean Bridge – a proposal that is, thankfully, still securely filed away or, hopefully, lost for all time. Across Rannoch the old military road keeps to the higher ground to avoid the many bogs that would have bedevilled a lower route.

This is probably the most remote spot on the West Highland Way; a perfect place for a break beneath great craggy summits, scree-riven gullies and the far hills of Achaladair.

The continuation starts through a small gathering of pine before beginning an unrelenting uphill haul to the first of two high points. Here, on the threshold of the vast Coire Ba, the British watershed is crossed for the penultimate time before the route eases down, past Lochan Mhic Pheadair Ruaidhe, to reach the splendidly turbulent **River Bà**. ◄

A short way on from Bà Bridge the track passes, on the left, the remains of Bà Cottage, surely one of the most isolated shielings imaginable, tucked away close by the Allt Creagan nam Meann. A hundred or so strides further and you pass a track, not all that evident, that leads out across the southern slopes of **Beinn Chaorach** to the A82, a marginally shorter way of reaching the road in an emergency than continuing along the Way. ◄

This is the original line of Caulfield's military road.

Steadily, the route rises again for its final crossing of the watershed, which it does not far from a prominent cairn, perched on the hillside to the left and dedicated

to the memory of Peter Fleming, brother of novelist Ian Fleming, who died nearby in 1971.

Buachaille Etive Mor from Black Rock

Now the track becomes less consistent, curves round the massive sprawling flanks of **Meall a'Bhuiridh**, and starts descending below the White Corries to join

RANNOCH MOOR

There is about the whole of this crossing of Rannoch Moor one peculiar and delightfully idiosyncratic aspect, which is the complete absence of any moment when suddenly the scenery becomes wonderful or stunning or breathtaking. Between Loch Tulla and Glen Coe it seems that every step of the way you are part of the scenery and the scenery is part of you. No amount of clever words will ever suffice to describe the experience; you must see it for yourself and form your own impression.

The landscape is also mightily enhanced by a host of lochs and lochans of all shapes and sizes that add constantly changing colour to the scene, from the darkest blacks to the brightest blues. In the breeding season, the lochs are visited by many species of wildfowl, including black-throated divers, the comparatively rare red-throated divers and greenshanks. Much of the area was once concealed within the great Caledonian pine forest, the

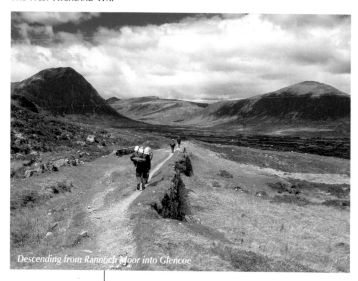

Descending from Rannoch Moor into Glencoe

Old Wood of Caledon, which formerly extended from Glen Coe to Braemar and from Glen Lyon to Glen Affric. Then it was home to rather more lethal forms of wildlife than at present, a place where brown bear, wild boar and wolves were to be found, along with the freebooters who sought sanctuary in the forest.

Much of the great Caledonian pine forest was destroyed by intentional fire and felling, firstly between the ninth and 12th centuries, and later between the 15th and 18th centuries. The first period of forest fires was instigated mainly by the Vikings and warring clans; the latter by the English and Scots who felled the woodlands for use in iron smelting and to root out wolves and freebooters. There are now very few remnants of that ancient forest, although some are to be found around Loch Tulla and yet more at the Black Wood of Rannoch.

Today, crossing the moor is all a far cry from those hazardous days when much depended on your skill in coping with difficult and dangerous terrain, and understanding the secret ways of the mountains and moors. It is along the West Highland Way, and this traverse of Rannoch in particular, that is as close as you can get to being at one with the hills. Make the most of it.

the chairlift access road near **Blackrock Cottage**. Here the Way turns right and marches out to rejoin the A82, briefly, as it crosses the busy road and presses on down a degenerating surfaced track that leads unerringly to the King's House Hotel. ▶

For the record, King's House is the hotel, while Kingshouse is the area around it.

The story of the **King's House Hotel** goes back perhaps 200 years or more. Certainly, in spite of its remoteness, it was at a key location along the highland drove roads – a fact readily recognised both by the government of the day and those potential innkeepers who were expected to man it. As a result, the innkeeper, seemingly loathe to take on such an isolated responsibility, ran the premises rent-free and received a substantial government grant for his efforts.

By all accounts, however, the innkeeper's efforts were often not much to write home about. One traveller who visited the hotel in 1791 described it as having 'not a bed fit for a decent person to sleep in nor any provisions but what are absolutely necessary for the family'. A surveyor of military roads in 1802 complained that it had 'more the appearance of a hog stye than an Inn', while Dorothy Wordsworth, who later had pleasant things to say about the Inveroran Hotel, found the King's House 'a wretched place – as dirty as a house after a sale on a rainy day'. JHB Bell in *Bell's Scottish Climbs* describes conditions at the King's House as 'primitive', where you could 'smell the bacon frying through a hole in the floor' or occasionally had to 'put up an umbrella in bed if the weather was wet'.

So, of the King's House you make what you will. It cannot be avoided, unless you keep on walking. It's not at all like that today.

SOUTHBOUND: KINGSHOUSE TO BRIDGE OF ORCHY

Distance	12 miles (19.2km)
Total ascent	1335ft (407m)
Total descent	1615ft (493m)
Walking time	5–6 hours
Terrain	Surfaced lanes lead to the base of the White Corries, from where a broad track eases upwards and out onto the expanse of Rannoch Moor; exposed with no shelter. The track is never in doubt and leads out to Forest Lodge, where a road comes in from Bridge of Orchy. A hillside final stage can be avoided by sticking to the road.
Accommodation	Inveroran, Bridge of Orchy

The day that strikes across the eastern slopes of Black Mount, the countless feeder burns of the River Bà and the western edge of Rannoch Moor is one of inspiration. Even on a bleak day, there is a magnificent presence about this long wilderness trek.

The day begins from **Kingshouse** by walking out along an old roadway to cross the A82 and continuing beyond it to pass the idyllically set **Blackrock Cottage**. Shortly after passing the cottage, bear left at a waymark, away from the access road to the Black Mount ski resort, and soon stride out across superb moorland – a knucklebone, heathery landscape of lochs and lochans, burns and rivers. Much of the area was once concealed within the great Caledonian pine forest, the Old Wood of Caledon, which formerly extended from Glen Coe to Braemar and from Glen Lyon to Glen Affric.

Initially, the Way follows the course of Caulfield's highway, but twice departs from it, taking a slightly lower line. Quite quickly the route rises to an obvious watershed, west of **Beinn Chaorach**. Close by, just off the Way to the right, stands a prominent cairn perched on the hillside. It is dedicated to the memory of Peter Fleming, brother of novelist Ian Fleming, who died nearby in a hunting accident in 1971.

Now a long, easy descent heads for the lonely outpost of Bà Cottage, these days much in need of a strong coat of paint or two. Beyond lies the undistinguished **Bà Bridge**, but for which the crossing of the River Bà could be troublesome. Easy walking ensues as Wayfarers stride across the edge of Rannoch Moor, with the bulk of the Black Mount summits commanding the western skyline. But to the south it's the glint of Loch Tulla and the shapely summits east of Bridge of Orchy that beckon.

On the old military road from Màm Carraigh to Forest Lodge

At **Forest Lodge**, the Way reaches the end of a surfaced road, crossing the Abhainn Shira at **Victoria Bridge** and, shortly, the Allt Tolaghan issuing from Gleann Fuar, from where it's a short walk to the Inveroran Hotel. William and Dorothy Wordsworth, in company with a south-bound cattle drove, stayed at the Inveroran Hotel in September 1803, although they were less than complimentary about the food.

At the Inveroran Hotel, a clear track rises onto Màm Carraigh, offering a splendid viewpoint in all directions. On a clear day, this is definitely the way to go; on less hospitable days, you may opt to follow the road, which adds to the distance, but avoids the ascent across the ridge above.

A final descent through woodland leads out onto the road at the rear of the **Bridge of Orchy** Hotel.

STAGE 6
Kingshouse to Kinlochleven

Start	King's House Hotel (NN 259 546)
Finish	River bridge, Kinlochleven (NN 187 620)
Distance	8¾ miles (14km)
Total ascent	1525ft (465m)
Total descent	2290ft (697m)
Walking time	4–5hrs
Terrain	There's a good path throughout this section, which traverses the mountain passes at the eastern end of Glen Coe, sticking to the old military road throughout, and climbs the Devil's Staircase before a long descent to remote Kinlochleven.
Accommodation	Kinlochleven

The next stage on the Way leads towards the great maw of Glen Coe (also often written as one word) – a glen made eternally famous (or would infamous be more appropriate?) by tales of the massacre of Glencoe (1692), so well and often poignantly described by John Prebble in *Glencoe*. His book, and likewise John Buchan's *The Massacre of Glencoe*, are essential reading for anyone who wishes to absorb the essence and menace of the highlands, and the story of Glen Coe in particular. The tale reflects an unhappy period in highland life, when most members of the Clan MacDonald were slaughtered by a body of soldiers under Captain Campbell after 12 days of professed friendship, all because of the clan chief's loyalty to the exiled James VII, which brought about a belated submission of the chief and his clan to William and Mary.

The crossing to Kinlochleven is comparatively short, beginning with a stretch across the lower slopes of Beinn a'Chrùlaiste, which provides a fine view of that great icon of Glen Coe, Buachaille Etive Mòr. This peak first came into view below White Corries on the way down from Rannoch Moor and largely dominates the scene until the route disappears over the Devil's Staircase. Thereafter a fairly relaxing route ensues, teasing a way around the eastern end of the north-eastern Glen Coe summits.

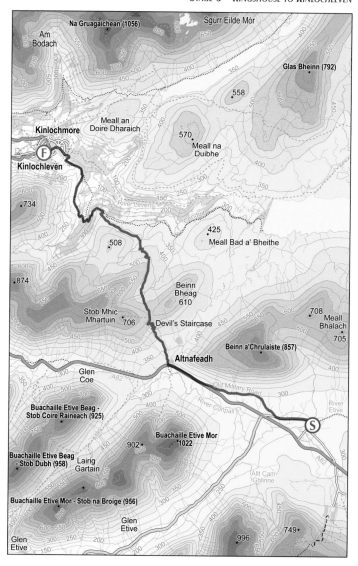

At Kingshouse

The setting of Kingshouse can be eerie or romantic according to your mood or companions.

From the King's House Hotel, take the surfaced lane crossing a bridge spanning the **River Etive** and passing by a camping area to a T-junction. Turn left, still on the surfaced lane, and keep along it to a gate and waymark well before rejoining the A82, and there turn right off the lane onto the old military road once more. ◀

Buachaille Etive Mòr is a summit, now owned and managed by the National Trust for Scotland, that has inspired generations of rock climbers since the days (and before) when WH Murray wrote 'the most striking moment was turning a corner of the road and seeing the great shape, black and intimidating, suddenly spring up in the moor. I had never seen a hill like it before and my breath was taken away from me.' He is, of course, describing the vision Wayfarers will receive, at a more leisurely pace, as they approach White Corries.

Everything Murray says about Buachaille Etive Mòr is true. The sudden appearance of the mountain as you begin the long run into Glen Coe is always an impressive and stirring sight. He goes on

to describe 'cliffs dove-grey and terracotta', adding that only from a distance is the Buachaille black.

Buachaille Etive Mor looms darkly at the entrance to Glencoe

Having left the surfaced lane at the gate, a rough track now rises onto the moor to begin an up-and-down traverse below the slopes of **Beinn a'Chrùlaiste**, with the forward view and that backwards to the summits of Black Mount always inspiring.

Gradually the track descends to cross a roadside fence and run parallel on a graded track with the A82 for a short distance and heading for the cluster of pine trees at Altnafeadh. Another fence crossing leads on to a path that gradually descends to road level, passing around sheep pens, as the great glen, Lairig Gartain, between Buachaille Etive Mòr and its sibling Buachaille Etive Beag eases into view. Eventually the path does come down to the road, and for a brief but hazardous distance the Way runs beside the A82. Shortly, as it reaches **Altnafeadh**, the Way leaves the road, dipping to the right and crossing the Allt na Féithe by a wooden footbridge, and then rises into heather and grass moorland at a waymark sign.

A good path rises across the moorland above Altnafeadh – moorland that may well have hosted grazing cattle in the days when Altnafeadh was a regular halt on the droves to the trysts at Falkirk and Crieff. Now it can sometimes see droves of a different order, those of laden Wayfarers bound for Kinlochleven. The route steadily gains height and brings improving views of the summits of Glen Coe and Black Mount, with the latter now becoming more distant.

Finally, with zigzags taking the sting out of the tail of the ascent, cross a cairned gap between **Beinn Bheag** and **Stob Mhic Mhartuin**, the highest point of the West Highland Way at 1798ft (548m).

GLEN COE

Setting aside its nefarious history and the blemishes that modern tourism have inflicted upon it, this remains a superlative glen – long, steep-sided, rugged, dark and mysterious – rising from the often turbulent waters of countless burns and rivers. In the Gaelic tongue the name signifies 'glen of weeping', yet in spite of any lyricism heaped upon it, it was regarded by Lord Macaulay in his *History of England* as '...the most dreary and melancholy of all the Scottish passes – the very Valley of the Shadow of Death'.

It is not clear whether, in making this comparison, Lord Macaulay had actually visited all the other Scottish passes, but he was far from happy with Glen Coe. 'Mists and storms brood over it through the greater part of the finest summer,' he wrote, 'and even on those rare days when the sun is bright, and when there is no cloud in the sky, the impression made by the landscape is sad and awful. Mile after mile the only sound that indicates life is the faint cry of a bird of prey from some storm-beaten pinnacle of rock.'

On a clear day, the view from the gap is outstanding – especially to the north, where walkers have their first glimpse of Ben Nevis, Carn Mor Dearg and the Mamores. Ahead and below lies a great boggy bowl drained by the Allt a'Choire Odhair-bhig, which feeds into the River Leven not far from the dam on the Blackwater Reservoir.

Before plunging down to the Allt a'Choire Odhair-bhig, the Way takes a relaxing moment at the top of the **Devil's Staircase**.

In spite of a poor reputation, the ascent of the **Devil's Staircase** out of Glen Coe is not at all difficult. The 'road' was probably constructed around 1750 by Major Caulfield's force, and it seems likely that it was the troops that gave the upper section of the route its name. Certainly it is only the top, zigzagging section that is properly called the Devil's Staircase, although the name seems to have been purloined by the whole stretch from Altnafeadh. What is intriguing about the Devil's Staircase route is why it came into being at all, since Caulfield could so easily have gone around the hills to the east and avoided the climb altogether. Both this pass and, further on, the Lairig Mor, were finally abandoned for military purposes in 1785, when the longer but easier road through Glen Coe to the ferry at Ballachulish was introduced.

On the descent, it's as if the delights of the earlier part of the Way are being forgotten and a distinctly new stage entered upon. Grass and heather, punctuated by bouldery outcrops, predominate as a rocky path sweeps down to the burn before slipping across the northerly end of a narrow ridge, Sron a'Choire Odhair-bhig. ▶ There's little choice of route along this stretch, so walkers can saunter or race along as they wish, although in poor visibility this is no place to explore away from the path. ▶

Having crossed the tip of Sron a'Choire Odhair-bhig, the Way continues to cross Allt a'Choire Odhair-mhoir and presses on to bring into view the huge black pipelines that traverse the hillsides from the reservoir. At one point the Way loops in a south-westerly direction to cross the Allt Choire Mhorair in a birch-wooded glen, by a bridge, before resuming its journey to Kinlochleven.

On the approach to Kinlochleven, as the path runs beside black water pipes, it is deflected right, behind the aluminium works, to a bridge across the **River Leven**. Beyond the bridge it runs into the edge of a housing estate at **Kinlochmore**. A short way along the road, the Way leaves the road on the left for a constructed pathway

If followed westwards this would rise onto the narrow and spectacular Aonach Eagach ridge – not a place for casual exploration!

Quite a few of the navvies working on the reservoir are known to have perished along this stretch as they lost their way in bad conditions.

through woodland, not far from the river, and rises on a pathway on the right just as it reaches the road bridge (B863) through **Kinlochleven**. A slanting track leads up to the road and an information panel.

SOUTHBOUND: KINLOCHLEVEN TO KINGSHOUSE

Distance	8¾ miles (14km)
Total ascent	2290ft (697m)
Total descent	1525ft (465m)
Walking time	4–5 hours
Terrain	A gradual climb on a good path leads out of Kinlochleven, and steadily works a way to a mountain threshold above the so-called Devil's Staircase, from where a path plunges downwards into the eastern end of Glen Coe. Wild and remote going throughout the section.
Accommodation	Kingshouse

The crossing to the eastern end of Glen Coe is virtually all uphill as far as the bealach at the top of the Devil's Staircase between Stob Mhic Mhatuin and Beinn Bheag. Thereafter a straightforward descent leads to the A82 at Altnafeadh, from where an elevated stretch along the old military road leads to Kingshouse. This is a remote and rugged stretch, where the sense of isolation is heightened by a ring of superb mountain summits.

The onward route leaves **Kinlochleven** at a signpost just on the north side of the River Leven and follows a path through **Kinlochmore** to a bridge spanning the river. Across this, and once free of the aluminium works that dominate this village, a brief climb leads to a gentler gradient as the route heads for the Allt Choire Mhorair, tumbling through a birch-wooded glen and crossed by a bridge.

Once more on Caulfield's military road, the route presses on steadily to cross the Allt a'Choire Odhair-mhoir and round the tip of Sron a'Choire Odhair-bhig – a north-easterly ridge thrown down from the Glen Coe wall. Simple plodding gradually leads to the bealach between **Stob Mhic Mhatuin** and **Beinn Bheag** – at 1798ft (548m), the highest point on the West Highland Way.

Now the Way tumbles down the so-called **Devil's Staircase** to reach the edge of Glen Coe at **Altnafeadh**. Here, opposite the inspiring bulk of

The King's House at Kingshouse

Buachaille Etive Mòr, walkers briefly join the busy A82 – but soon leave it, on the left, for the line of the military road. This continues a little above the glen before descending to a gate giving onto a minor road that leads to the rear of the King's House Hotel.

STAGE 7

Kinlochleven to
Fort William

Start	River bridge, Kinlochleven (NN 187 620)
Finish	Nevis Bridge, Fort William (NN 112 742)
Distance	14 miles (22km)
Total ascent	2325ft (710m)
Total descent	2325ft (710m)
Walking time	7–8hrs
Terrain	A steep climb out of Kinlochleven leads into the hidden valley of Lairig Mor, with a broad track running on to Nevis Forest. Throughout the Lairig Mor section, the path is crossed by many burns issuing from the hillsides. Most are simple and easy to negotiate, and others have footbridges, but in times of spate one or two could prove troublesome. The route through the forest is rough in places, with a few tiring undulations, but then, once the high point it attained, it's all downhill to Glen Nevis, and a final road walk out to conclude the day.
Accommodation	Fort William

The remaining stage to the end of the Way begins with a steady but steep climb from Kinlochleven to gain Lairig Mor – a fascinating and wholly unexpected glen that is the preserve only of pedestrians and estate workers, concealed behind the high ridged summits of Mam na Gualainn and Beinn na Caillich. Beyond the glen the route swings northwards, leaving the military road near Blar a'Chaorainn to start its final rush to the embrace of Glen Nevis and journey's end. This is quite a long stage, with no refreshments and little shelter. Be sure, therefore, that you are fully prepared and provisioned before leaving the many facilities of Kinlochleven behind.

KINLOCHLEVEN

With parts of the township forever pitched in shade during the winter months and set so far from modern through-routes, it is not surprising that Kinlochleven has earned an unenviable reputation. WH Murray certainly was not enamoured of the place, describing it as 'The ugliest [township] on two thousand miles of Highland coast, this through an industry of high social value employing nearly a thousand men and women.' He does, however, relent a little as his view widens, commenting that 'Kinlochleven nestles at the foot of the Mamore Forest, a range of spiry mountains seen well from the high road of approach. The mountain scale is great enough to absorb the town into itself, so that ... wood, loch, and mountain wholly dominate the scene, the town shrinking to merely wart-like dimension.'

Kinlochleven, which today very much thrives on the passage of Wayfarers, at the turn of the 19th century was little more than two independent settlements – Kinlochmore and Kinlochbeg – until expansion came with the building of the British Aluminium Company.

For many years the road journey northwards lay through Kinlochleven or by way of the Ballachulish ferry, which although regular was of limited capacity, and it was often quicker to drive around the loch. In 1975 all that changed with the opening of the Ballachulish bridge.

Resuming the journey from **Kinlochleven**, walk down the road, heading roughly north-west, out of the town, as far as a waymark and signpost on the right ('Footpath to Glen Nevis by the Lairig'). The Way continues by rising steadily as a stony track through birch scrub until, at a waymark, the path forks. Branch left here to cross a burn, and press on steeply through more scrub to reach a surfaced lane serving Mamore Lodge.

Mamore Lodge, now a hotel, perches high up on the flank of Am Bodach. It was formerly a shooting lodge used by King Edward VII, and it has for years provided a base for walkers venturing into the Mamores along the many deer-stalking tracks and disused roads that criss-cross the mountainsides.

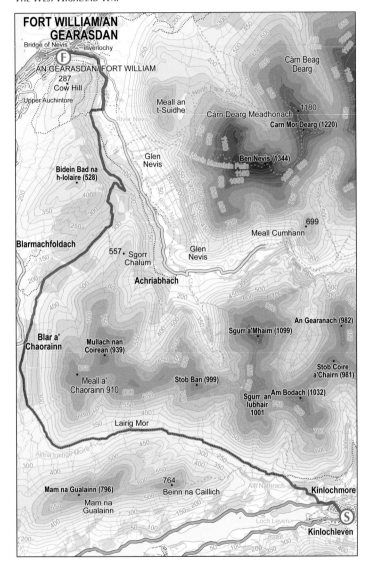

FORT WILLIAM/AN GEARASDAN

Bridge of Nevis
Inverlochy
F
AN GEARASDAN/ FORT WILLIAM
287
Cow Hill
Upper Auchintore

Càrn Beag Dearg

Allt Daim

North Face Path

Meall an t-Suidhe

Càrn Dearg Meadhonach
1180
Carn Mor Dearg (1220)

River Nevis

Ben Nevis Mountain Path

Ben Nevis (1344)

Glen Nevis

Bidein Bad na h-Iolaire (528)

River Nevis

699

Meall Cumhann

Blarmachfoldach

557 Sgorr Chalum

Glen Nevis

Achriabhach

An Gearanach (982)

Sgurr a'Mhaim (1099)

Blar a' Chaorainn

Mullach nan Coirean (939)

Stob Coire a'Chairn (981)

Meall a' Chaorainn 910

Stob Ban (999)

Sgurr an lubhair 1001

Am Bodach (1032)

Lairig Mor

Allt na Lairige Moire

Mam na Gualainn (796)

764
Beinn na Caillich

Allt Nathrach

Kinlochmore

Mam na Gualainn

Loch Leven

S
Kinlochleven

118

Cross the hotel access and resume the upward plod through more woodland. After a while the path climbs to a junction with a track that has risen from the valley road, and continues ascending in zigzags for some distance until, finally, clear of the woodland scrub, it rejoins the military road at a waymark. Turn left and initially begin a gentle descent.

Once the military road is reached, the walking becomes much easier and the onward route never in question, leaving Wayfarers free to take in a superb panorama that embraces the Munros behind Ballachulish and pinnacled sections of the Aonach Eagach, probably the finest continuous ridge-walk on mainland Britain. The ridge then leads the eye to the Pap of Glencoe (Sgorr na Ciche), effectively and neatly closing the view down Loch Leven to the west.

Walkers have plenty of opportunity to concentrate on their surroundings as the Way progresses steadily towards a high point beyond the **Allt Nathrach**, following which it descends to the first of two deserted steadings, Tigh-na-sleubhaich. The second, a short distance further on, is Lairig Mor, and both are evocative reminders of a distant, lonely and hard-won existence that few these days could countenance in any meaningful way. ▸

The Lairig Mor is a wild landscape of considerable beauty, and it is not difficult to imagine the hardships faced by people who lived here – especially if it's raining when you arrive!

Tigh-na-sleubhaich, Lairig Mor

Cattle would be brought to these high mountain pastures for grazing during the summer months, as they still are in parts of the French Alps and the Pyrenees.

In 1645, after the Battle of Inverlochy, MacDonalds from Montrose's army pursued a number of Argyll's defeated forces through this area, and the cairn is said to represent the spot where the MacDonalds gave up the chase. and the Pyrenees.

The track continues stonily past both buildings, traversing superb and remote hill country along the southern flank of the western Mamores. Finally, it rounds the southern flanks of **Mullach nan Coirean** and its southwestern satellite, **Meall a'Chaorainn**, to run northwards with the Allt na Lairige Moire. For most of the way through the glen the path is now descending, and passes the site of more old shielings. ◂

As walkers descend the track, and just before reaching Blar a'Chaorainn, a large cairn is encountered at the side of the track. ◂

There has been widespread felling of trees in this area in the past decade, and the forest of old no longer exists other than as stubby and untidy reminders of the trees that once held sway here. The Way continues through this desolation to intercept a wide forest trail close by an information panel. Here, the Way finally abandons Caulfield's road close by the site of **Blar a'Chaorainn** toll house, of which virtually nothing remains.

In the glen to the side at this point lies **Lochan Lùnn Dà-Bhrà**. In ancient times, Macbeth, King of the Scots from 1040 to 1057, is said to have resided on an island in the lochan, probably a crannog. Like many lakes throughout Britain, Lochan Lùnn Dà-Bhrà is said to be inhabited by a monster – a mythical creature that leaves the lochan to kill grazing stock.

ROUTE NOTE

Anyone feeling especially weary or running short of time should consider remaining with the road – not an unacceptable proposition – which provides a much easier stage into Fort William. Certainly walkers get a good view of Loch Linnhe and Fort William by pursuing this option, which is not available to the main route. From the junction, not far from Lochan Lùnn Dà-Bhrà, the road down into Fort William is surfaced.

The final stage involves some rough and trying walking through extensive woodland before it gives in

Passing through the Glen Nevis forest

gracefully and slips down into Glen Nevis for the final stretch of road walking and increasing urbanisation to Bridge of Nevis.

The Way branches right from the old military road just beyond the information panel and rises on a track through a clear-felled area, which shortly it leaves at a deer gate/fence. It then continues as a stepped pathway over and around a small hillock before coming down to another cleared area at a deer gate/fence. Quickly, it runs down to cross the Allt Coire a'Mhuilinn by a footbridge, flanked by goat willow and birch, before passing on to reach more mature larch and pine.

On the way, there is a view of Meall an t-Suidhe and **Ben Nevis** that could well represent another day's walking for the very fit. The Ben is not showing you its most attractive face from this angle, quite the opposite, but it never fails to impress with its sheer bulk and domination of all the surrounding countryside.

The track now undulates through more forest, ultimately to descend a constructed flight of steps to a footbridge over a burn beside a large boulder. Beyond that, it presses on more or less horizontally for some time before climbing steeply to the top edge of the forest. Here the Way breaks out from the forest and onto a wide forest trail.

A new path has been created to give access to **Dùn Deardail** – a vitrified fort dating back to the Iron Age. It's not far to go to reach it, so if you have the time and interest, do so. The rubble walls of the fort were fused into a glassy mass by fire, which may have occurred accidentally or as a result of attack by raiders.

The forest trail, now clear of trees, steadily descends and shortly reaches a lower trail, which leads downwards into the glen. After some time, at a sharp bend, are found a couple of waymarks. One identifies the most direct route to Glen Nevis Youth Hostel, for those bound for an overnight stay there. The other keeps left for a little longer until it, too, meets a waymark that takes walkers off the forest trail and down an easy path through trees to a gate and then out to meet the glen road. All that remains is to turn left and simply follow the road the remaining distance to the end of the Way at **Bridge of Nevis**.

Ben Nevis

122

On the way, you will pass a large boulder by the roadside – the so-called Wishing Stone or Stone of Counsel (Clach Comhairle), to which various legends have been ascribed, including one which avows that at times the whole rock rotates and settles down again. Anyone encountering the stone while in its rotation (it only occurs on one night of the year – my money is on Hogmanay!) will get answers to any three questions put to the stone.

Well done! I hope you enjoyed your West Highland Way as much as I have.

CLIMBING BEN NEVIS

After building up your strength on the Way you may find the challenge of climbing Ben Nevis, Britain's highest summit, irresistible. But it's a long climb. Most walkers will take 3–4 hours for the ascent, and 2–3 hours for the descent. Using the route described below, the total distance is 16km/10 miles, and the total ascent is 4275ft (1303m). Take OS Explorer map 392, or Harveys Ben Nevis and Glencoe Mountain Map.

Unless you're staying at the Glen Nevis Youth Hostel, walkers take a taxi from Fort William to Achintee Farm (NN 126 731), and start the ascent from there. If you start from Glen Nevis the distance is a little shorter, but the height gain rather more. The route is clear throughout, but very rocky all the way, and virtually every step is an uphill one. You begin by a long curving route around the bulk of Meall an t-Suidhe (pronounced 'Mellantee') that feeds into a steep-sided ravine housing Red Burn. Easier ground appears just south of Lochan Meall an t-Suidhe, bringing some respite from the uphill work. But shortly you gain a foothold on the Ben itself, doubling back from the Lochan Meall an t-Suidhe path to begin a series of wide zigzags that gradually guide you upwards towards the summit plateau. When the gradient finally relaxes, it heralds the first of a number of false summits before the summit trig comes into view.

At the start of the descent in poor visibility, it is vital to navigate accurately to avoid the gullies that cut into the north face of the mountain, or over-compensating, and straying too far south of the correct line onto the steep and dangerous slopes above Glen Nevis.

SOUTHBOUND: FORT WILLIAM TO KINLOCHLEVEN

Distance	14 miles (22.5km)
Total ascent	2325ft (725m)
Total descent	2325ft (725m)
Walking time	7–8 hours
Terrain	A gentle stroll into Glen Nevis leads to a broad forest trail ascent through Nevis Forest to the northern edge of Lairigmor. A broad trail leads southwards and then east following an old military road, before abandoning it for a steep descent to Kinlochleven. There may be some difficult burn crossing after prolonged wet weather
Accommodation	Kinlochleven

Compared to the first day on the Way in the south to north direction, this reverse direction requires rather more effort, although it is not overly demanding. After a brief walk out of Fort William, the route makes a challenging and undulating climb through the confines of Nevis Forest. Once above and free of the forest (much of which has been cleared), however, the route is sheer delight all the way to Kinlochleven, allowing you to enjoy the largely inaccessible quarters of Lairigmor, the Big Glen.

Conventionally, the northern end of the Way is marked by a signpost at **Nevis Bridge**, and from here Wayfarers stride alongside the road into Glen Nevis. Ahead and slightly to the left is the bulk of Meall an t-Suidhe, squat before the even greater bulk of Ben Nevis.

Fell-racing mankind contrive to run up and down Meall an t-Suidhe from the Town Park just outside Fort William in under 28mins (men) and 34mins (women), and dismiss Ben Nevis, the highest mountain in Britain, in 1hr 25mins and 1hr 43mins respectively. They can complete the West Highland Way – on which you are about to spend a week or so – in under 16 hours (men) and 17 hours 30mins (women). Such levels of fitness and stamina are unlikely to be needed by regular Wayfarers – so, other than as a mark of respect, spare no further thought for such endeavours, and start along the route into Glen Nevis.

As the route continues into the glen, so the distinctive profiles come into view of Sgùrr a'Mhàim and Stob Bàn, further up the glen. Along the way pass a large boulder by the roadside, the so-called Wishing Stone or Stone of Counsel (Clach Comhairle) to which various legends have been ascribed.

Beyond the cemetery and the visitor centre, and just 1¼ miles (2.2km) into the walk, leave the road at a waymark (NN 122727) and follow a narrow path towards mixed woodland, entered by a gate. Climb easily for a short while to meet a broad forest trail, which now leads roughly in a southerly direction, ascending steadily all the while and making great loops as it works its way ever upwards. On the way it is joined by a route that comes up from the youth hostel in the glen. Eventually a high point is reached, and there is much evidence of continuing forest clearance hereabouts.

Now keep an eye open for a waymark on the left, at a point where a descending path leaves the forest trail (roughly at NN 124 704). What seems like an unduly long forest interlude now ensues, away from the openness of forest trails and much more closely flanked by trees. On the way pass Dùn Deardail, a vitrified fort. A diversion to the fort might be contemplated, but walkers would be better advised to preserve their energy for the pleasures of what is to come.

A number of broad, deep undulations are a characteristic of this stretch and lead to a large boulder beside the path, near a bridge. Beyond, a flight of constructed steps takes the path higher, still maintaining its switchback fashion until, finally, it breaks free of the forest high above the unseen Allt nan Gleannan. A clear path now continues through an extensive area that has been cleared – without this you would still be trudging through forest. The path is never in doubt, tackles a few streams and deer gates, and finally arrives at **Blar a'Chaorainn**, at the head of a minor road arriving from Fort William.

To the west, the road runs on briefly to the farms at Lundavra beside the beautiful Lochan Lùnn Dà-Bhrà. An information panel relates some of the history of the area. There used to be a toll house here; that minor road from Fort William is actually a road of some significance, as it is one of Major Caulfield's military roads. Here, at Blar a'Chaorainn, this historic highway is joined, and, fittingly, it will be the Way's companion, off and on, for some days to come.

Cross a forest trail at this point, keeping to a clear path that soon rises to a large cairn marking a significant moment in a 17th-century battle. Ahead now Lairig Mor awaits, a most sumptuous glen, clean of line, flanked by shapely hills, and blessed with a great track drawing walkers on. The only wrong you can do here is to hasten. Between this point and Kinlochleven,

Elevated view of Kinlochleven

the way is still long but extravagantly beautiful, and a relaxed pace will see you comfortably through.

After 2 miles (3km) of gentle uphill walking, the track turns the south-western flanks of **Mullach nan Coirean** and begins a long and steady descent, passing the ruined crofts at Lairigmor and Tigh-na-sleubhaich – the latter rather more substantial than the former. Just beyond Tigh-na-sleubhaich the Way crosses a threshold as the ground starts to slip towards Kinlochleven. There's a more pronounced descent now, but still not excessive, just a gradual decline that gives easy walking.

Caulfield's road passes to the north of Kinlochleven, but, before then, there's a clear point where the West Highland Way takes its leave (NN 172 630) and descends for a brief skirmish with birch woodland, crossing the access lane to Mamore Lodge, now a hotel, high up on the flank of Am Bodach. This was formerly a shooting lodge used by King Edward VII, and it has for years provided a base for walkers venturing into the Mamores.

Across the lane, the path continues down through birch to reach the glen road a short distance out of **Kinlochleven**.

APPENDIX A
Useful contacts

Tourist boards

All enquiries for tourist information in Scotland are now handled through the main Visit Scotland centre in Edinburgh.

Visit Scotland
Level 3
Ocean Point
194 Ocean Drive
Edinburgh
EH6 6JH
Tel 0845 22 55 121
info@visitscotland.com
www.visitscotland.com

Visitor and information centres

Balloch
Old Station Building
Balloch Road
Balloch
Dunbartonshire
G83 8LQ
Open April–early Oct
Tel 08707 200 607
www.visitscottishheartlands.com

National Park Gateway Centre
Loch Lomond Shores
Ben Lomond Way
Balloch
Dunbartonshire
G83 8LQ
Open April–Oct
Tel 01389 751031
www.lochlomondshores.com

Balmaha
National Park Centre
Balmaha
G63 0JQ
Tel 01360 870470
www.visitscotland.com

Fort William
15 High Street
Fort William
PH33 6DH
Open April–Oct
Tel 0845 22 55 121
www.visithighlands.com

Glen Nevis Visitor Centre
Glen Nevis
Fort William
Inverness-shire
PH33 6PF
Open April–Oct
Tel 01397 705922

Pack-carrying services

These services tend to operate between Easter and the end of October; call for services outside these dates.

A1–AMS Scotland
22 Redhills
Lennoxtown
G66 7BL
Tel 01360 312 840 or 07872 823 940
info@amsscotland.co.uk
www.amsscotland.co.uk

A2B Travel-Lite
The Iron Chef
5 Mugdock Road
Milngavie
Glasgow
G62 8PD
Tel 0141 956 7890 or 07778 966 592
info@travel-lite-uk.com
www.travel-lite-uk.com

Ginger Routes
Cameron Farm
Alexandria
Glasgow
G83 8QZ
Tel 07577 463 613
mail@gingerroutes.com
www.gingerroutes.com

Sherpa Van Project
3 Bedford Road
London
W4 1JD
Tel 01748 826917
info@sherpavan.com
www.sherpavan.com

Public Transport

For up-to-date information about timetables ring Traveline Scotland on 0871 200 22 33 (24/7). If you have internet access you can also visit their website at www.travelinescotland.com/welcome.do or download the free Traveline app to your smartphone or iPhone.

Trains

Detailed timetables of rail services from across Britain are available at:

The Trainline
www.thetrainline.com

National Rail Enquiries
Tel 0845 748 4950
www.nationalrail.co.uk

ScotRail
Tel 0344 811 0141
www.scotrail.co.uk

Buses

Glasgow to Milngavie:
First Bus
Tel 0870 608 2608

Milngavie to Drymen:
Aberfoyle Coaches
Tel 0844 567 5670

Balloch to Balmaha:
HAD Coaches
Tel 0870 608 2608

Fort William to Kinlochleven:
Stagecoach
Tel 01397 702373

Glasgow to Fort William:
Scottish Citylink
Tel 0870 550 5050

Waterbus service on Loch Lomond

Scheduled ferry services between the eastern and western shores of Loch Lomond afford walkers the option of booking accommodation on the western shore and returning to the Way the following day to continue the route. The ferries allow walkers to enjoy shorter stretches of the Way as they also provide a link to public transport on the A82. All vessels on ferry services have bar, tea and coffee facilities. Dogs welcome.

All services are provided in partnership with Sweeney's Cruises (tel 01389 752 376; www.sweeneyscruises.com),

Cruise Loch Lomond (tel 01301 702356; www.cruiselochlomond.co.uk) and the Ardlui Hotel (tel 01301 704 243; www.ardlui.com). The timetable varies annually, but is available to download on the Park website (www.lochlomond trossachs.org).

Taxis

If you need to bail out for any reason, there are some local taxi services, as well as the public transport options.

Drymen Taxi Service
Tel 01360 660 077

West Highland Way Taxis
Tel 07024 089 089
www.west-highland-way-transport.co.uk

West Highland Taxis
(Fort William, Glencoe and Kinlochleven)
Tel 01855 831495
www.westhighlandtaxis.com

Ambassador Taxis (Milngavie)
Tel 0141 956 2956
www.ambassador-taxis.co.uk

24/7 Cars (Crianlarich)
Tel 01838 300 307
www.247taxis.co.uk

Alistair's Taxis (Ballachulish)
Tel 01855 811 136
www.alistairstaxis.co.uk

Alistair's Taxis (Fort William)
Tel 01397 252 525
www.alistairstaxis.co.uk

Other organisations

Loch Lomond and the Trossachs
National Park
Carrochan
Carrochan Road
Balloch
G83 8EG
Tel 01389 722 60
info@lochlomond-trossachs.org
www.lochlomond-trossachs.org

Ordnance Survey
Romsey Road
Maybush
Southampton
SO16 4GU
Tel 08456 05 05 05
customerservices@ordnancesurvey.co.uk
www.ordnancesurvey.co.uk

The Mountaineering Council of
Scotland
The Old Granary
West Mill Street
Perth
PH1 5QP
Tel 01738 493 942
info@mountaineering-scotland.org.uk
www.mountaineering-scotland.org.uk

The National Trust for Scotland
Herniston Quay
5 Cultins Road
Edinburgh
EH11 4DF
Tel 0131 458 0200
information@nts.org.uk
www.nts.org.uk

Scottish Natural Heritage
Great Glen House
Leachkin Road
Inverness
IV3 8NW
Tel 01463 725 000
enquiries@snh.gov.uk
www.snh.org.uk

Scottish Rights of Way and Access
Society
24 Annandale Street
Edinburgh
EH7 4AN
Tel 0131 558 1222
info@scotways.com
www.scotways.com

Scottish Youth Hostels Association
7 Glebe Crescent
Stirling
FK8 2JA
info@syha.org.uk
www.syha.org.uk
For reservations:
Tel 0345 293 7373
reservations@syha.org.uk

APPENDIX B
Accommodation

This list is selective. If you find accommodation listed here that is closed or unwelcoming to walkers, or know of suitable accommodation that we have left out, please let us know. Similarly, if you are an accommodation provider who would like adding to the list, or taking off the list, do get in touch.

The latest version of this list can be downloaded from the Cicerone Press website (www.cicerone.co.uk/857/accommodation) and there is also a useful listing on www.west-highland-way.co.uk.

Information about accommodation throughout the entire route is also available at Milngavie Information Point (13 Main Street, Milngavie G62 6BJ, info@westhighlandwayinfo.com, www.westhighlandwayinfo.com).

There are a number of accommodation-booking companies that offer discounted rooms, but it is sometimes cheaper to contact hotels and B&Bs direct.

Milngavie

Allander (B&B)
28 Buchanan Street
Milngavie
G62 8AN
Tel 0141 956 5258

Best Foot Forward @ West View (guest house)
1 Dougalston Gardens South
Milngavie
G62 6HS
Tel 0141 956 3046
www.bestfootforward.eu.com

Premier Inn (hotel)
103 Main Street
Milngavie
G62 6JQ
Tel 0871 527 8428
www.premierinn.com

Drymen

Ashbank (B&B)
1 Balmaha Road
Drymen
G63 0BX
Tel 01360 660 449
www.ashbank-drymen.co.uk

Bolzicco's (B&B)
8 Old Gartmore Road
Drymen
G63 0DP
Tel 01360 660 566
www.bolziccos.com

Buchanan Arms (hotel)
Drymen
G63 0BQ
Tel 01360 660 588
www.buchananarms.co.uk

Braeside (B&B)
5 Main Street
Drymen
G63 0BP
Tel 01360 660 989
www.braeside-drymen.co.uk

Cairndhu (B&B)
3 Endrick Way
Croftamie
Drymen
B63 0DH
Tel 01360 660 730

Croftburn Cottage (B&B)
Croftamie
Drymen
G63 0HA
Tel 01360 660 796
www.croftburn.co.uk

Glenalva (B&B)
Stirling Road
Drymen
G63 0AA
Tel 01360 660 491
www.glenalva-drymen.co.uk

Green Shadows (B&B)
Buchanan Castle Estate
Drymen
G63 0HX
Tel 01360 660 289
www.bedandbreakfastlochlomond.net

Hill View (B&B)
4 The Square
Drymen
G63 0BL
Tel 01360 661 000

Kip in the Kirk
(B&B and bunk room)
The Old Church
11 Stirling Road
Drymen
G63 0BW
Tel 07734 394 315
www.kipinthekirk.co.uk

Mulberry Lodge (B&B)
Gateside
Drymen
G63 0DW
Tel 01360 660 215
www.mulberrylodge.co.uk

The Drymen Inn (bar-restaurant with rooms)
5 Stirling Road
Drymen
G63 0BW
Tel 01360 660 123
www.thedrymeninn.com

The Hawthorns (guest house)
The Square
Drymen
G63 0BH
Tel 01360 661 222
www.hawthorns-drymen.com

Shandon Farmhouse (B&B)
Drymen
G63 0EA
Tel 01360 661 328
shandonfarmhousebedandbreakfast.simpl.com

Balmaha

Arrochoile (B&B)
Balmaha
G63 0JG
Tel 01360 870 231
www.whw-bb-lochlomond.com

Balmaha House (B&B and bunkhouse)
Balmaha
G63 0JQ
Tel 01360 870 218
www.balmahahouse.co.uk

Bay Cottage (B&B)
Balmaha
G63 0JQ
Tel 01360 870 346
www.lochlomond-cottage.co.uk

Milarrochy Bay (campsite, Loch Lomond side)
Drymen
G63 0AL
Tel 01360 870 236
www.campingandcaravanningclub.co.uk

Oak Tree Inn (inn and bar-restaurant with coffee shop)
Balmaha
G63 0JQ
Tel 01360 870 357
www.theoaktreeinn.co.uk

Passfoot Cottage (B&B)
Balmaha
G63 0JQ
Tel 01360 870 324
www.passfoot.com

Sallochy Bay
Rowardennan
G63 0AW 01360 870 142
http://scotland.forestry.gov.uk
Campsite

Rowardennan

Anchorage Cottage (B&B)
Rowardennan
G63 0AW
Tel 01360 870 394
www.anchoragecottage.co.uk

Ben Lomond Bunkhouse
Rowardennan
G63 0AR
Tel 0131 458 0305
www.nts.org.uk

Rowardennan Hotel
Rowardennan
G63 0AR
Tel 01360 870 273
www.rowardennanhotel.co.uk

Rowardennan Lodge (SYHA youth hostel)
Rowardennan
G63 0AR
Tel 01360 870 259
www.syha.org.uk

The Shepherd's House (B&B)
2 Forestry Cottages
Rowardennan
G63 0AW
Tel 01360 870 105
www.theshepherdshouse.co.uk

Inversnaid

Inversnaid Bunkhouse (with bistro and some camping)
Inversnaid
FK8 3TU
Tel 01877 386 249
inversnaid.com

Inversnaid Hotel
Inversnaidby
Aberfoyle
FK8 3TU
Tel 01877 386 223
www.lochsandglens.com

Garrison Farm (B&B)
Inversnaid
FK8 3TU
Tel 01877 386 341

Inverarnan

Beinglas Farm (camping cabins, B&B chalets, campsite, bar and restaurant)
Inverarnan
G83 7DX
Tel 01301 704281
www.beinglascampsite.co.uk

Drovers Inn
Inverarnanby
Ardlui
G83 7DX
Tel 01301 704 234
www.thedroversinn.co.uk

Crianlarich

Craigbank (guest house)
Main Street
Crianlarich
FK20 8QS
Tel 01838 300 279
www.craigbankguesthouse.com

Crianlarich Hotel
Crianlarich
FK20 8RW
Tel 01838 300 272
www.crianlarich-hotel.co.uk

Crianlarich Youth Hostel (SYHA)
Station Road
Crianlarich
FK20 8QN
Tel 01838 300 260
www.syha.org.uk

Ewich House (B&B)
Strathfillan
Crianlarich
FK20 8RU
Tel 01838 300 300
www.ewich.co.uk

Glenardran House (B&B)
Crianlarich
FK20 8QS
Tel 01838 300 236
www.glenardran.co.uk

Riverside (guest house)
Tigh na Struith
Crianlarich
FK20 8RU
Tel 01838 300 235
www.riversideguesthouse.co.uk

Tyndrum

By the Way (campsite, wigwams, hostel)
Lower Station Road
Tyndrum
FK20 8RY
Tel 01838 400 333
www.tyndrumbytheway.com

Dalkell Cottage (guest house)
Lower Station Road
Tyndrum
FK20 8RY
Tel 01838 400 285
www.dalkell.com

Glengarry House (guest house)
Tyndrum
FK20 8RY
Tel 01838 400 224
www.glengarryhouse.com

Pine Trees Leisure Park (campsites with camping huts)
Tyndrum
FK20 8RY
Tel 01838 400 349
www.pinetreescaravanpark.co.uk

Strathfillan Wigwams (wigwams, some camping, farm shop)
Auchtertyre Farm
Tyndrum
FK20 8RU
Tel 01838 400 251
www.wigwamholidays.com

Bridge of Orchy

Bridge of Orchy Hotel
Argyll
PA36 4AD
Tel 01838 400 208
www.bridgeoforchy.co.uk

West Highland Way Sleeper (unisex bunk rooms)
Bridge of Orchy railway station
PA36 4AD
Tel 07778 746 600
www.westhighlandwaysleeper.co.uk

Inveroran

Inveroran Hotel
Bridge of Orchy
PA36 4AQ
Tel 01838 400 220
www.inveroran.com

Glen Coe

Glencoe Mountain Resort (camping, microlodges, bar and café)
White Corries
Kingshouse
Glencoe
PH49 4HZ
Tel 01855 851 226
www.glencoemountain.co.uk

King's House Hotel
Glen Coe
Argyll
PH49 4HY
Tel 01855 851 259
www.kingshousehotel.co.uk

Kinlochleven

Allt na Leven (guest house)
23–24 Leven Road
Kinlochleven
PH50 4RP
Tel 01855 831 366
www.bedandbreakfastkinlochleven.co.uk

Blackwater Hostel (private hostel with campsite)
Lab Road
Kinlochleven
PH50 4SG
Tel 01855 831 253
www.blackwaterhostel.co.uk

Edencoille (guest house)Garbhein Road
Kinlochleven
PH50 4SE
Tel 01855 831 358
www.kinlochlevenbedandbreakfast.co.uk

Highland Getaway (B&B, bar and restaurant)
28 Leven Road
Kinlochleven
PH50 4RP
Tel 01855 831 506
www.highlandgetaway.co.uk

MacDonald Hotel (with camping and cabins)
Fort William Road
Kinlochleven
PH50 4QL
Tel 01855 831 530
www.macdonaldhotel.co.uk

Tigh na Cheo (guest house)
Garbhein Road
Kinlochleven
PH50 4SE
Tel 01855 831 434
www.tigh-na-cheo.co.uk

Fort William

Achintee Farm (B&B and hostel)
Achintee
Glen Nevis
Fort William
PH33 6TE
Tel 01397 702 240
www.achinteefarm.com

Ben Nevis (guest house)
Nevis Bridge
Glen Nevis
Fort William
PH33 6PF
Tel 01397 708 817
www.bennevisguesthouse.co.uk

Burnlea (B&B)
Achintore Road
Fort William
PH33 6RN
Tel 01397 706 307
www.burnleahouse.com

Glen Nevis Caravan and Camping Park
PH33 6SX
Tel 01397 702 191
www.glen-nevis.co.uk

Glen Nevis Youth Hostel (SYHA)
PH33 6SY
Tel 01397 702 336
www.syha.org.uk

Gowan Brae (B&B)
Union Road
Fort William
PH33 6RB
Tel 01397 704 399
www.gowanbrae.co.uk

Premier Inn (hotel)
Loch Iall an Aird
Fort William
PH33 6AN
Tel 0871 527 8402
www.premierinn.com

Travelodge (hotel)
High Street
Fort William
PH33 6DX
Tel 0871 984 6419
www.travelodge.co.uk

APPENDIX C
Further reading

JHB Bell, *Bell's Scottish Climbs* (Gollancz, 1988)

Donald Bennet, *The Southern Highlands*, 3rd revised edn (Scottish Mountaineering Trust, 1992)

Mary B Bruce, *The Buchanans: Some Historical Notes* (Stirling District Libraries, 1995)

ARB Haldane, *The Drove Roads of Scotland* (Birlinn Ltd, 2015)

George Rowntree Harvey, *A Book of Scotland* (A and C Black, 1949; reprint, 1953)

Brian Paul Hindle, *Roads, Tracks and their Interpretation* (Batsford, 1993)

Maurice Lindsay, *The Lowlands of Scotland: Glasgow and the North* (Robert Hale, 1979)

GF Maine (ed), *A Book of Scotland* (Collins, 1950 and 1972)

WH Murray, *The Companion Guide to the West Highlands of Scotland*, 7th edn (Collins, 1977); *Mountaineering in Scotland and Undiscovered Scotland*, new edn (Baton Wicks Publications, 1997)

John Prebble, *Glencoe* (Penguin Books, 1978)

Sir Walter Scott, *Rob Roy* (Penguin Classics, 1995)

William Taylor, *The Military Roads in Scotland*, new edn (House of Lochar, 1996)

Nigel Tranter, *The Story of Scotland*, 4th revised edn (Neil Wilson Publishing, 2012)

Ronald Turnbull, *The West Highland Way* (Frances Lincoln, 2010); *Not The West Highland Way* (Cicerone, 2010)

NOTES

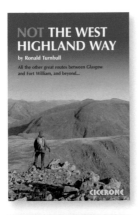
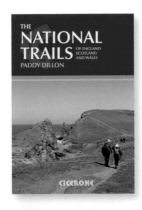
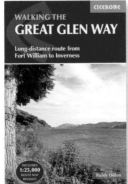
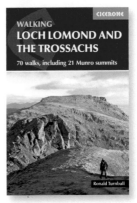

LISTING OF CICERONE GUIDES

Walking on the Gower
Welsh Winter Climbs

DERBYSHIRE, PEAK DISTRICT AND MIDLANDS

Cycling in the Peak District
Dark Peak Walks
Scrambles in the Dark Peak
Walking in Derbyshire
White Peak Walks:
  The Northern Dales
White Peak Walks:
  The Southern Dales

SOUTHERN ENGLAND

20 Classic Sportive Rides
  in South East England
20 Classic Sportive Rides
  in South West England
Cycling in the Cotswolds
Mountain Biking on the
  North Downs
Mountain Biking on the
  South Downs
North Downs Way Map Booklet
South West Coast Path Map
  Booklet – Minehead to St Ives
South West Coast Path Map
  Booklet – Plymouth to Poole
South West Coast Path Map
  Booklet – St Ives to Plymouth
Suffolk Coast and Heath Walks
The Cotswold Way
The Cotswold Way Map Booklet
The Great Stones Way
The Kennet and Avon Canal
The Lea Valley Walk
The North Downs Way
The Peddars Way and Norfolk
  Coast Path
The Pilgrims' Way
The Ridgeway Map Booklet
The Ridgeway National Trail
The South Downs Way
The South Downs Way
  Map Booklet
The South West Coast Path
The Thames Path
The Thames Path Map Booklet
The Two Moors Way
Walking in Cornwall
Walking in Essex
Walking in Kent
Walking in London
Walking in Norfolk
Walking in Sussex
Walking in the Chilterns
Walking in the Cotswolds
Walking in the Isles of Scilly
Walking in the New Forest

Walking in the North
  Wessex Downs
Walking in the Thames Valley
Walking on Dartmoor
Walking on Guernsey
Walking on Jersey
Walking on the Isle of Wight
Walking the Jurassic Coast
Walks in the South Downs
  National Park

BRITISH ISLES CHALLENGES, COLLECTIONS AND ACTIVITIES

The Book of the Bivvy
The Book of the Bothy
The C2C Cycle Route
The End to End Cycle Route
The End to End Trail
The Mountains of England and
  Wales: Vol 1 Wales
The Mountains of England and
  Wales: Vol 2 England
The National Trails
The UK's County Tops
Three Peaks, Ten Tors

ALPS CROSS-BORDER ROUTES

100 Hut Walks in the Alps
Across the Eastern Alps: E5
Alpine Ski Mountaineering
  Vol 1 – Western Alps
Alpine Ski Mountaineering Vol 2
  – Central and Eastern Alps
Chamonix to Zermatt
The Tour of the Bernina
Tour of Mont Blanc
Tour of Monte Rosa
Tour of the Matterhorn
Trail Running – Chamonix and
  the Mont Blanc region
Trekking in the Alps
Trekking in the Silvretta and
  Rätikon Alps
Trekking Munich to Venice
Walking in the Alps

PYRENEES AND FRANCE/ SPAIN CROSS-BORDER ROUTES

The GR10 Trail
The GR11 Trail – La Senda
The Pyrenean Haute Route
The Pyrenees
The Way of St James – France
The Way of St James – Spain
Walks and Climbs in the Pyrenees

AUSTRIA

The Adlerweg
Trekking in Austria's Hohe Tauern

Trekking in the Stubai Alps
Trekking in the Zillertal Alps
Walking in Austria

SWITZERLAND

Cycle Touring in Switzerland
The Swiss Alpine Pass Route –
  Via Alpina Route 1
The Swiss Alps
Tour of the Jungfrau Region
Walking in the Bernese Oberland
Walking in the Valais
Walks in the Engadine –
  Switzerland

FRANCE

Chamonix Mountain Adventures
Cycle Touring in France
Cycling the Canal du Midi
Écrins National Park
Mont Blanc Walks
Mountain Adventures in
  the Maurienne
The Cathar Way
The GR20 Corsica
The GR5 Trail
The GR5 Trail – Vosges and Jura
The Grand Traverse of the
  Massif Central
The Loire Cycle Route
The Moselle Cycle Route
The River Rhone Cycle Route
The Robert Louis Stevenson Trail
The Way of St James –
  Le Puy to the Pyrenees
Tour of the Oisans: The GR54
Tour of the Queyras
Tour of the Vanoise
Vanoise Ski Touring
Via Ferratas of the French Alps
Walking in Corsica
Walking in Provence – East
Walking in Provence – West
Walking in the Auvergne
Walking in the Cevennes
Walking in the Dordogne
Walking in the Haute Savoie:
  North
Walking in the Haute Savoie:
  South
Walks in the Cathar Region
Walking in the Ardennes

GERMANY

Hiking and Biking in the
  Black Forest
The Danube Cycleway Volume 1
The Rhine Cycle Route
The Westweg